# Becoming New

# Becoming New

*Finding God within Us
and in Creation*

⥲

## Anselm Grün and Leonardo Boff

Translators

**Patricia C. Bellm and Robert A. Krieg**

ORBIS ✦ BOOKS
**Maryknoll, New York 10545**

The publishing arm of the Maryknoll Fathers and Brothers, Orbis Books seeks to explore the global dimensions of the Christian faith and mission, to invite dialogue with diverse cultures and religious traditions, and to serve the cause of reconciliation and peace. To learn more about Orbis Books, please visit our website at OrbisBooks.com.

Copyright © 2019 by Orbis Books.

Originally published as *Neu Denken – Eins Werden: Gott erfahren im Menschen und in der Welt* © 2017 Vier-Türme GmbH, Verlag, 97359 Münsterschwarzach Abtei.

English translation published by Orbis Books, Box 302, Maryknoll, NY 10545-0302.

Manufactured in the United States of America
Manuscript editing and typesetting by Joan Weber Laflamme.

**Library of Congress Cataloging-in-Publication Data**

Names: Grün, Anselm, author.
Title: Becoming new : finding God within us and in creation / Anselm Grün and Leonardo Boff ; translators Patricia C. Bellm and Robert A. Krieg.
Other titles: Neu Denken-Eins Werden. English
Description: Maryknoll : Orbis Books, 2019. | Includes bibliographical references.
Identifiers: LCCN 2019004339 (print) | LCCN 2019018892 (ebook) | ISBN 9781608337958 (e-book) | ISBN 9781626983311 (pbk.)
Subjects: LCSH: Spirituality—Christianity. | Experience (Religion)
Classification: LCC BV4501.3 (ebook) | LCC BV4501.3 .G82513 2019 (print) | DDC 248—dc23
LC record available at https://lccn.loc.gov/2019004339

# Contents

### Part One
### THE DIVINE IN US
### ANSELM GRÜN

v

**Part Two**
**THE DIVINE IN US AND THE UNIVERSE**
**LEONARDO BOFF**

# Foreword
# by the German Publisher

I was delighted when we received the inquiry from our Brazilian publishing partner, Editora Vozes, asking whether we would envision a common book that both publishing houses would release at more or less the same time. This book would be written by the two most well-known spiritual authors of our countries: Fr. Anselm Grün and Leonardo Boff.

I anticipated that this project would be challenging, all the more as the authors would hardly be able to discuss the theme on which we ultimately agreed. In particular, it would be difficult for them to exchange ideas; the distance between Brazil and Germany is too vast and the authors' agendas too full.

Nevertheless, readers will likely have the sense that the authors are actually engaging in a dialogue, and that, although they are approaching the same question—namely, where and how we are to find and experience God—from differing perspectives and with differing emphases, they reach quite similar conclusions and insights.

The specific question at the heart of the text by Anselm Grün concerns how to discover God in a human being, in myself but also in the other, in my neighbor. In contrast, Leonardo Boff places the emphasis more on the discovery of God in the existence of the universe, beginning with the Big Bang and ending with the smallest creature that lives on our planet.

Despite these different starting points, both authors are amazingly in agreement, particularly concerning the essence of God. They hold that God is not the One who exists apart from the world as the Wholly Other, but rather that God is found precisely in the world—in a human being and also in animals and plants. God is not, however, identical with the world. As Leonardo Boff says, God remains the great "nameless Mystery" that eludes the human imagination and categories. Therefore, God can never to be fully grasped by human beings. Yet I can encounter God whenever I do something with love or where love is present. The two authors also agree on this: the essence of God is love; indeed, God is love. God is simultaneously mysterious as well as powerful and unfathomable. Wherever love reigns, we can experience God with all of our senses, and we—as individual human beings and as the entire cosmos—can become one with God.

It is a great delight to accompany in this book these two authors on their different paths as they arrive at their respective insights.

BROTHER LINUS EIBICHT
VIER-TÜRME PUBLISHERS
MÜNSTERSCHWARZACH, GERMANY

# Preface
## by the Translators

In the Foreword by the German Publisher, Brother Linus Eibicht notes that this book's Part One is the work of Anselm Grün, OSB, in Germany, and that Part Two is the work of Leonardo Boff in Brazil. Implicit here is that Part One was written in German by Grün and translated by Markus A. Hediger into Portuguese for the book's publication in Brazil. Part Two was penned in Portuguese by Boff, after which it was translated into German by Sarah Pasquay for the book's publication in Germany.

This English translation is primarily rendered from the German text: *Neu denken—Eins werden: Gott erfahren im Menschen und in der Welt* (Münsterschwarzach: Vier-Türme-Verlag, 2017). Yet, this English edition has gained greater faithfulness to the book's Part Two by working also with the Portuguese text: *Divino em nós* (Petrópolis: Editora Vozes, 2017).

For the sake of accuracy this English translation includes full references to the literature to which Anselm Grün and Leonardo Boff refer. For example, it gives specific references to the texts by Augustine of Hippo,

Albert Einstein, and Pierre Teilhard de Chardin, SJ, which Grün and Boff quote.

Finally, this English translation conveys the differing spiritual traditions of Anselm Grün and Leonardo Boff. That is, Part One's vocabulary reflects the spirituality of Saint Benedict of Nursia (480-547). It emphasizes how human beings may meet God in prayerful solitude, in what Grün—drawing on the thought of C. G. Jung—refers to as one's "inner room of stillness." Part Two's vocabulary conveys the spiritual orientation of Saint Francis of Assisi (1181–1226). It highlights how human beings may encounter God in creation, thus living what Leonardo Boff—drawing on Pope Francis's encyclical *Laudato Si'*—calls an "ecological spirituality." As a result, this book shows that while the spiritual orientations of Anselm Grün and Leonardo Boff differ, they are also complementary. As Brother Linus Eibicht observes, this book invites readers to walk the Benedictine and also the Franciscan paths to God.

The translators remain grateful to Robert Ellsberg, publisher of Orbis Books, for inviting them to make this rich spiritual book available to English-speaking readers.

PATRICIA C. BELLM AND ROBERT A. KRIEG

# Part One

# The Divine in Us

**ANSELM GRÜN**

**Anselm Grün**

FATHER ANSELM GRÜN, a Benedictine monk at Münsterschwarzach Abbey, is one of the most widely read Christian authors of today, reaching an audience across all denominations and nationalities. Dom Anselm has written over 380 books, which have been translated into thirty-four languages and have sold around seventeen million copies to date.

Anselm Grün, born in 1945, spent his childhood with his parents and six siblings in Munich. The close relationship with his family shaped him very much. To this day, his siblings are important anchor points in his life. He has developed various book projects with his brother Michael Grün, his sister Linda Jarosch, and his niece, Andrea Larson, who lives in the United States.

In 1964, Anselm Grün graduated from a German secondary school and entered the novitiate at the Benedictine Münsterschwarzach Abbey in the same year. He studied philosophy, Catholic theology, and business administration in St. Ottilien, Rome, and Nuremberg respectively.

In 1976, Anselm Grün authored his first book titled *Purity of the Heart*. He became acquainted with the art of human conduct from the Rule of Benedict of Nursia. Furthermore, having been inspired by the psychology of Carl Gustav Jung, he has rediscovered the tradition of the desert fathers, whose meaning he connects with the knowledge of modern psychology.

In 1977, he was appointed cellarar (financial director) of the Münsterschwarzach Abbey, responsible for the economic management of the Abbey with its twenty

companies. During this time he initiated the moderniza-
tion and opening of the monastery and equipped the
abbey for the challenges and issues of the twenty-first
century.

In his more than two hundred courses and lectures
per year throughout Germany and abroad, he addresses
the needs and questions of the people. He is interested
in what really moves people today. Living spirituality
in everyday life, finding the right balance between one's
work and private life, being mindful of creation, but
also dealing with oneself are all important topics in his
writing and lectures.

Anselm Grün leads numerous courses and work-
shops for prominent companies like Audi, Daimler,
BMW, and Bayer Pharmaceuticals, among others. In
Hong Kong and Taiwan he leads courses regularly for
Christian traders/employers. He also gives lectures in
Mexico, Brazil, Chile (for example, at the Catholic
University in Santiago and the National University in
Valparaiso), Argentina, Colombia, Singapore, Korea,
and East Malaysia, as well as nearby communities and
at the guesthouse of the Münsterschwarzach Abbey.

Finally, he is honored to provide spiritual and
psychological counsel to priests and to religious and
ecclesiastical workers during times of personal crisis or
upheaval. In fact, in 2018, his book *Midlife* as a Spiritual Challenge was recommended reading for priests
by Pope Francis.

# 1.

# God,
# the Unfathomable Mystery

When I have said in my previous publications that God dwells in us, I have used the language of mysticism, focusing more on the individual human being in whom God dwells. Of course, I have never regarded a human being as an isolated being but always as someone who lives in a community with others and who—as Saint Benedict teaches in his *Rule*—is an attentive steward of creation. As I have read Leonardo Boff's text about the Divine in us and the universe and also studied some of his other recent books, it has dawned on me that I must always see human beings as part of the cosmos. Further, when I speak of God in human beings, I cannot neglect our connection to the cosmos. Human beings bear the

14-million-year-old stardust from the beginning of the world and our cosmos. They have much in common with the surrounding matter and the living reality of flora and fauna. Even their brains show many similarities to those of animals. In the words of Leonardo Boff, the human brain is

> organized on three levels: the reptilian brain, which first emerged some 220 million years ago and corresponds to our instinctive actions; this is surrounded by the limbic brain, which began to emerge some 125 million years ago and corresponds to emotions, affectivity, and a sense of care; and, finally, the cerebral cortex, only three million years old, which provides the ability for conceptualization and abstract thought.[1]

When I speak today of the Divine in human beings, I think also of our deep, inner connection with the entire cosmos. The God within us is always the One who unites us with the entire cosmos, for we are part of it. The God who dwells within human beings also dwells in everything that exists.

My engagement with the insights of Leonardo Boff has compelled me to widen my point of view. In this book we speak of the Divine in us and the universe.

---

[1] Mark Hathaway and Leonardo Boff, *The Tao of Liberation: Exploring the Ecology of Transformation* (Maryknoll, NY: Orbis Books, 2009), 312.

Yet, the mystics speak of God in us, meaning the personal God, the Father of Jesus Christ, and our Father and our Mother. However, as I see it, this is no contradiction. For me, God is always both: God is personal and beyond-personal. The "Divine" stresses rather the beyond-personal aspect, that is, other-than-personal.

I am indebted to Karl Rahner for my theology. He called God the "Absolute Mystery."[2] "Mystery" is also a rather beyond-personal term for God. However, Karl Rahner was convinced—and in this regard I join with him—that in this unfathomable and indescribable mystery of God we encounter a "Thou."

Thus, I always see in the Divine also the God who speaks to me, who meets me as a "Thou." At the same time, I know, however, that I must not form concrete images of God. I must not think of God as a human counterpart.

Many people run into problems with their personal images of God when they are confronted by suffering. They ask how God as Father or Mother can allow a child to die. Suffering challenges us to crack open our images of God as a person—a concept that is quite often too narrow—and to consider the other aspect of God: God as the unfathomably deep Mystery, God as the Power that permeates everything, God as the Love that brings forth everything and that connects everything. Both views are legitimate. They open the window

---

[2] Karl Rahner, *Foundations of Christian Faith*, trans. William V. Dych (New York: The Seabury Press, 1978), 44–89.

through which we can behold God who is beyond all of our images and constructs, beyond the juxtaposition of our personal and supra-personal views. At the same time, God envelopes and faces us as the unfathomably deep Mystery of Love.

When we speak in this book of the Divine, we are not denying that God is a person. Rather, we are using a wider language so that we can also reach people who are not at home in the Christian faith. However, we always also think of God as a person. The Greek church fathers described God not with our notion of person but with *hypostase* (hypostasis). *Hypostase* characterizes a particular existence in contrast to a general essence. Literally, the word *hypostase* means "that which stands under." The church fathers developed this concept when they wanted to understand the mystery of the triune God. God is one God in three distinct *hypostasei*, concrete existences, which means that the Divine always encounters us in the concrete. Therefore, in the Western tradition we have translated *hypostase* with the word *person.* Together with the Eastern theological tradition, we believe that God encounters us as "Thou," not only as universal Essence. Thus, when speaking of the Divine, we always also think of God as person, God as the Thou who speaks to us, to whom we pray, and with whom we have a relationship.

Using the term *Divine* instead of the term *God* can also lead to a misunderstanding. We speak sometimes of the Divine as though the Divine were our possession, belonged to us, enriched us, and increased our mental abilities. In doing so, we assume that we are already entirely one with the Divine and, therefore, no longer in need of human relationships. We flee into such grandiosity in order to avoid our human neediness. When we speak about the Divine, we must always remember that God remains sacrosanct, that we do not possess God but must approach this God or the Divine with reverence and piety. Reverence means to have no access to the Divine, but rather to step back and to let God be Mystery and to allow ourselves to be touched by the Divine. As Paul Tillich said, God is "what concerns us absolutely."[3]

In this book, we limit ourselves to speaking about the Divine that is in us, in our brother and sister, and in the natural world that surrounds us. Still, in this Divine there always resonates God's "Thou" who faces us. We cannot coopt the Divine that is already in us. However, like God, the Divine cannot be set aside. We cannot

---

[3] See Paul Tillich, *The Dynamics of Faith* (New York: Harper and Row, 1957), 1–3.

command the Divine. We can only receive the Divine in gratitude as a gift. In the words of Karl Rahner, God is the unfathomable Mystery that always and everywhere surrounds us and to which we are continuously oriented. For this reason we should not speak of human beings without speaking also of this Mystery that is in us and toward which we are heading. We should not speak of the Divine within us without thinking about the Divine that permeates the entire cosmos.

God is the mysterious Energy that has released the Big Bang and that drives the genesis of the cosmos, the formation of life, evolution, and history, and that interconnects everything. God is the unifying Power without which the cosmos would fall apart.

I am writing only of God in human beings. However, the thoughts Leonardo Boff develops later are already considered here. Both aspects belong together. Both describe the mystery of the human being who is part of the cosmos—or, as Leonardo Boff puts it, the human being in whom the cosmos began to think and to marvel and to understand itself.[4]

---

[4] Hathaway and Boff, *The Tao of Liberation*, 316–17.

# 2.

# The Longing to Encounter God as Person

In conversations I often hear Christians complain about having lost their relationship with God. Previously, they were able to pray to God as to a friend. They shared everything with God. They had a sense of God's love and were very familiar with God. Now, however, they no longer sense God's presence.

Now, this God seems to be so very far from them. They long to reestablish the earlier familiar relationship. Yet, I cannot offer them a fix on how they can revive this feeling. My first question for people who approach me with this kind of issue is, "Do you actually have a sense of yourself?" We cannot sense God when we are not in touch with ourselves. We cannot build a relationship with God when we are not relating well to ourselves. Many people refuse to accept that they might have lost touch with themselves or are not relating well to themselves. However, after a longer conversation, they often recognize that they have become strangers to themselves, indeed, estranged from themselves.

This estrangement also involves their relating with their environment. To have a sense of oneself always means to feel oneself to be embodied. And, because of that, I sense my environment in and through my body. Human beings are taken from the earth. I am in contact with myself only when I sense also this earthiness being a part within me. The Latin word for a human being, *homo*, has its etymological root in *humus*, which means "soil." This meaning is at play also in the Hebrew word for a human being, *adam*, which originated from the Hebrew word *adama*, "earth." For this reason Leonardo Boff has translated the name of the Bible's first human being, Adam, with the word "Earthling."[1] Therefore, only a human being who senses nature is able to sense God or, as the Buddhists say, has empathy for all that exists—with the stones, the plants, the animals, and other human beings. Whoever exists without a relationship with self and nature loses as well the relationship with God. Then we don't sense God, who has become strange to us.

---

[1] Mark Hathaway and Leonardo Boff, *The Tao of Liberation: Exploring the Ecology of Transformation* (Maryknoll, NY: Orbis Books, 2009), 319.

The first way to sense God again involves, therefore, sensing myself again. I try to feel my breath, to let my breath take me to the ground of my soul. I listen to the inner impulse of my soul, which leads me beyond myself and the ordinary of everyday life. The early church fathers taught us that we cannot experience God unless we are ready to encounter ourselves honestly and to experience and sense ourselves as we are. Cyprian of Carthage writes: "How can you ask to be heard of [by] God when you do not even hear yourself? Do you expect the Lord to be mindful of you in your entreaties when you are not even mindful of yourself?"[2] If you yourself are not with you, how can you want God to be with you? If I am not at home with myself, then God cannot find me when God wants to come to me. To listen to oneself means to listen to one's true being, to come in touch with oneself. It also means, however, to listen to one's feelings and needs, to listen to that which stirs within. To listen to oneself, to come into touch with oneself and one's deepest needs, this is for Cyprian the necessary condition for coming into touch with God.

Evagrius Ponticus has formulated it similarly: "If you want to know God, know yourself first."[3] There is no awareness of God without self-awareness, and no

---

[2] Cyprian of Carthage, *St. Cyprian on the Lord's Prayer*, trans. T. Herbert Bindley (New York: Edwin S. Gorham, 1904), 62–63.

[3] Evagrius Ponticus, *The Praktikos Chapters on Prayer*, trans. John Eudes Bamberger, OCSO (Spencer, MA: Cistercian Publications, 1970), #86, 69.

encounter with God without me encountering myself. This happens as I am attentive to my feelings and thoughts. Another possible way to encounter myself is to ponder the question, Who am I? If I pose this question again and again and do not settle for quick answers, I will get a sense that questions about the true self will ultimately lead me to God, to the One who has created me, to the One who has formed a unique image of me.

Another obstacle to a personal encounter with God stems from a reproach against people of faith, a reproach made by the German philosopher Ludwig Feuerbach as well as by the psychologist Sigmund Freud. They sought to demonstrate that our views of God as father or mother are simply infantile projections. According to them, we project our desire for a perfect father or an always loving mother onto God and, ultimately, can remain stuck in our infantile stage in which we feel entirely dependent on a father and a mother.

There is certainly a kernel of truth in this reproach. There are people who project their infantile needs onto God. Later, they become disappointed when God's self-disclosure does not convey a loving father or an understanding mother but instead reveals an unfathomable God whom we do not understand and who often enough appears to be absent. God is more, however, than the projection of infantile desires. God is the One who, since the earliest times, has provoked philosophers and thinkers with this question: What will I find if I continue to search for the Essence of all being? Ultimately, I will come upon the unfathomable Mystery, which is more than the projections of human images, more specifically, the Mystery that is leading me to question myself. God is the One who persistently asks me, "Who are you?" Or, as God asked Adam, "Adam, where are you?" [Gen 3:9]. Similarly, God asks me, "Where do you stand? How do you understand yourself?"

The Swiss psychologist C. G. Jung presupposes that there is indeed a legitimate projection of our infantile longings onto God. However, this step means that we do not put God on the same level as our father and mother. Rather, using symbols, the libido—the energy of life—must be directed to a spiritual level. According to Jung, symbolic truth, "which puts water in place of the mother and spirit or fire in place of the father, frees the libido from the channel of the incest tendency, offers it a new gradient, and canalizes it into a spiritual form."[4] In this regard Jung calls symbols "transformers, their function being to convert libido from a 'lower' to a 'higher' form."[5] When a young man remains attached to his mother in an infantile manner, he shies away from life. He is haunted by anxieties. He has to separate from his mother, even though a longing for her will remain. Only when he directs this longing to a symbol can he mature from adolescence into adulthood.

---

[4] Carl Gustav Jung, *Symbols of Transformation*, 2nd ed., trans. R. F. C. Hull (Princeton, NJ: Princeton University Press, 1956), 226.
[5] Ibid., 232.

Therefore, when we no longer see God on the same level as a mother or a father, we can benefit from this redirection of the libido. We can become free from the bonds to our parents and be able to go our own way. However, we do not live without ties. We bind ourselves to God. The word *religion* means precisely that. The Latin word *religare* means "to bind, to tie." We do not live without ties, without responsibilities, abandoned. We are tied to God. And, we stand responsible to God. We answer God's call with our human existence.

Today, responsibility always also entails accepting responsibility for the care of the entire cosmos. The Jewish philosopher Hans Jonas understood responsibility as such: we are responsible not only for the consequences of our actions. We must also actively assume responsibility for the world.[6] We are responsible for whether the climate gets increasingly warmer and ultimately leads to the geozid, or we safeguard the cosmos as an enjoyable place for us.[7] Already, the Greek philosopher Aristotle understood the responsibility of a civic leader to include the concern for the continuation of human life into the future.

In spiritual counseling I often encounter people who have not yet taken the step of transforming their infantile wishes; rather, they continue to speak of God

---

[6] Hans Jonas, *The Imperative of Responsibility: In Search of an Ethics for the Technological Age*, trans. Hans Jonas with David Herr (Chicago: The University of Chicago Press, 1984).

[7] Translators' note: the term *geozid* refers to "the end of the earth's atmosphere."

as if God were a father and a mother. Their religious talk is more a projection of their childhood needs onto God and not a transformation of the energy of life into spiritual energy. Jesus did not say that God would give us only security and a sense of home. For Jesus, God is also the One who challenges us to go our own way. The man whom Jesus calls to follow him but who would like first to bury his father hears Jesus's harsh words: "Let the dead bury their own dead; but as for you, go and proclaim the kingdom of God" (Lk 9:60). We can speak correctly of God only when, within us, father and mother are dead, when we have been set free from being tied to them. Only then can we experience God in a new way as Father and Mother.

The longing to experience God as person, to encounter God personally, exists in us. It is not a sign of something infantile but corresponds to our essence as human beings. The image of God always also corresponds to one's self-image. Experiencing God as person is, therefore, the necessary condition to experiencing oneself as a person. Speaking only of the Divine runs the risk of ignoring one's own personality. One can feel united with everything without understanding oneself as a unique person. Yet, it is precisely as an individual that I am able to enter into relationships with other human beings. As such, I can feel united with nature and can experience union with God. This union is not a fusion with God; rather, it is a oneness as the union of two persons. The ancient dogmatic formulation of the Council of Chalcedon speaks of the union between us and God as "undivided and unconfused." We become one with God and the Divine. However, we remain human beings. We do not become commingled with the Divine.

The Old Testament's account of the burning bush in which Moses encountered God (Ex 2:23) is a beautiful image to express the council's teaching: overlooked, the withered bush grows at the margins. It is considered insignificant. Yet, it is in this bush of thorns that God appears as fire. The bush burns without being consumed. Each of us is the place where God's glory appears, where the fire of God burns. Still, we remain human beings. We remain matter; we remain the weary bodies that will fall sick and become old. Nevertheless, the divine fire burns in us. This is the Bible's promise: we are the place where God's glory shines forth for the entire cosmos.

# 3.

# God in Us

## *The Birth of God in Human Beings*

All of the Christian mystics are convinced that God dwells in us and speak of this by means of various images. They root their conviction in Jesus's words in the Gospel of John: "'Those who love me will keep my word, and my Father will love them, and we will come to them and make our home with them'" (Jn 14:23). In these words Jesus says that the Father and he himself dwell within us. In his death he will not only prepare a home for us with God in heaven, but he and God the Father already move in with us now and pitch a tent in us. The church fathers have used this verse from John's Gospel as one of many starting points for the doctrine of the triune God. God is communion; Father,

Son, and Holy Spirit are one, and still they are three
persons. Each one dwells in the other and permeates
the other. In order to express this reality, the church
fathers have developed the notion of *perichorese*, which
originally meant "mutual permeation." Leonardo Boff
translates this term as "to dance around together."[1] The
triune God is an eternal dance of One with each of the
Others. The triune God dwells in human beings. The
Trinity is an image used to convey that God draws us
into this dance of love. The triune God is an open God,
open to dwelling in human beings. Richard of Saint
Victor, one of the most important Paris theologians of
the twelfth century, holds that the essence of the triune
God is love.[2] He draws an analogy to the love between
two people, explaining that perfect love always requires
three persons: the lover, the beloved, and the third who
cherishes this love. The Father loves the Son who loves
the Father. The Holy Spirit is the communicated love,
the love that connects the Father and the Son. According to Richard of Saint Victor, the dwelling of the triune
God in human beings means that we are the dwelling

---

[1] Mark Hathaway and Leonardo Boff, *The Tao of Liberation: Exploring the Ecology of Transformation* (Maryknoll, NY: Orbis Books, 2009), 326–27.

[2] Mary T. Clark, "The Trinity in Latin Christianity," in *Christian Spirituality*, vol. 1: *Origins to the Twelfth Century*, ed. Bernard McGinn (New York: Paulist Press, 1985), 276–90. Dr. Mary T. Clark (d. 2014), an internationally respected scholar, was a member of the Society of the Sacred Heart (RSCJ) and taught at Manhattanville College, Purchase, New York.

place of the love that gives, the love that responds, and the love as gift that is given to us. The Holy Spirit divinizes our human love and makes us able to direct this love not only to God and human beings but also to the whole of creation. Thus, the indwelling of God in the human soul is not something that human beings keep for themselves. Rather, it opens them for others and the whole of creation, which is permeated with the love of the Holy Spirit. Mary T. Clark describes this understanding of spirituality: "Spiritual life is no flight from 'alone to the Alone,' but a relating to all in the threefold way of Father, Son, and Holy Spirit."[3] The triune God, who dwells in us, enables us to become one with everything that is because everything is permeated by the Spirit of God.

The mystics have described God's dwelling in human beings in various ways. Many church fathers draw on biblical texts such as the image of the Holy of Holies in the Letter to the Hebrews [9:1–28]. Connecting Greek and Jewish elements of faith, the author describes Christ as our "forerunner," who has proceeded us through death into "the inner shrine behind the curtain" (Heb 6:19–20). Behind the curtain is the Holy of Holies, to which only the high priest had access (Heb 9:3). Christ has entered into the Holy of Holies. However,

---

[3] Ibid., 288.

this Holy of Holies exists no longer in the Temple but in us. There, where Christ dwells in us, everything is *healed* and *made whole*. There is a room in each one of us that is off limits for other human beings. Even the noise of the world cannot enter this Holy of Holies. There everything is *holy*; everything is removed from the world. This room is God's dwelling place. And there, where God lives in us, we can be entirely ourselves. There, we come into contact with the *holiness* and *healing* in us.[4]

Another biblical image is that of the temple of God. In his First Letter to the Corinthians, Paul writes: "Or do you not know that your body is a temple of the Holy Spirit within you, which you have from God, and that you are not your own? For you were bought with a price; therefore glorify God in your body" (6:19–20). Our body is the dwelling place of the Holy Spirit. And with the Holy Spirit, God's beauty lives in us. When we become conscious of this, we experience ourselves and other people differently. We recognize the dignity of our body; it not only bears our soul, it is also the place in which God dwells.

The Gospel of John wants us to understand the expulsion of the merchants from the Temple as Christ entering into our market area and transforming it into

---

[4] Translators' note: The German text weaves together the words *heilig* and *geheilt*. The adjective *heilig* means "holy," and the verb *geheilt* means "healed," "made whole," and thus implies "saved." God's gifts of becoming "holy," *heilig*, and being "healed," *geheilt*, are interwoven in human life. These gifts are brought to us by Jesus Christ, *der Heiland*, usually translated as "the Savior," literally "the Bearer of health, wholeness."

the temple of God [Jn 2:13–25]. Jesus expels the inner noise of the merchants and moneychangers. He kicks out the oxen, sheep, and doves—that is, impulsiveness, excessiveness, and swirling thoughts—so that God's beauty can enter. Once God's beauty dwells in us, we come to know ourselves also as beautiful and experience the inner dignity and beauty of our body and soul.

A scripture verse that springs from the mysticism of Saint Paul has traditionally been associated with both the indwelling of God and also God's birth: "And it is no longer I who live, but it is Christ who lives in me" (Gal 2:20). Christ lives in me; he has become my true self. Still, at the same time, each of us can say: "Christ is being born in me. He is becoming my innermost reality." When Christ is born in us, he becomes our true self. Then we do not live out of our ego, but rather we live out of our innermost center. It is not our ego that lives but our true self.

C. G. Jung calls Jesus the archetype of the self. Jesus's message has touched human beings because it has awakened in them the archetypal image of the self. Christ gave people the hope of moving from an enclosed ego to an inclusive self. The self includes both conscious and also unconscious realms in the human soul. Jung also writes that Christ, as the archetype of the self, embraces the essence of the cosmos; thus, the self has always been connected with the whole cosmos.[5]

---

[5] Carl Gustav Jung, *Psychology and Religion: West and East*, 2nd ed., trans. R. F. C. Hull (Princeton, NJ: Princeton University Press, 1969), 156.

Time and again the church fathers describe the birth of God in the human soul and how every Christian, whether a man or a woman, is the mother of Christ. They often refer to Matthew 12:50: "For whoever does the will of my Father in heaven is my brother and sister and mother." Pointing to Mary as the preeminent example, the mystics of the Middle Ages interpret this biblical verse as referring to Christ's inner birth in the hearts of human beings; Christ was born in Mary but also in the soul of every Christian.

Each human soul is a maternal place in which God is born. Also, the heart is often described as the place where God's Word becomes incarnate in us. Clement of Alexandria writes how the *Logos* lives in us. Those who have the *Logos* living within them "receive the beautiful figure of the *Logos*, become beautiful themselves, for they become similar to God. Indeed, they become 'God,' because God intends this. Oh, Mystery Revealed: God in human beings, and human beings in God."[6] These are courageous words; God lives in the *Logos*, in the Son Jesus Christ, in our hearts, and makes us one with God. Thus we share in the beauty of God.

The late church fathers say that God becomes a human being so that human beings will become divine. And, in the divinization of human beings, the whole

---

[6] Clement of Alexandria, quoted in Hugo Rahner, "Die Gottesgeburt. Die Lehre des Kirchenväter von der Geburt Christi im Herzen des Gläubigen," *Zeitschrift für katholische Theologie* 59 (1935): 341. See Hugo Rahner, *Symbole der Kirche: Die Ekklesiologie der Väter* (Salzburg: O. Müller, 1964).

cosmos will also become divine. It is within this cosmic perspective that Leonardo Boff has interpreted the incarnation of God in Jesus Christ; in the human body of Jesus, God has, as it were, united the whole cosmos with his divine life.[7]

The church fathers view the birth of the eternal *Logos* from the Virgin Mary as an image of the spiritual birth of Christ in the heart of each human being. For Origen, the *Logos*—who is born in the human soul in baptism—must also grow in order to increasingly transform the human soul into the image of Christ. This transformation manifests itself in the virtues the human being learns from Jesus, and it eventually culminates in the beatific vision for which the Christian is destined.

The church fathers speak of the birth in baptism that has to continue day-after-day in the birth of the *Logos* in the human soul. This more and more transforms the actions, thoughts, and conversations of human beings, and it imbues them with the Spirit of Jesus. The teaching of the Greek church fathers culminates in the mysticism of Gregory of Nyssa. He writes:

This birth happens out of God alone. And, it develops as someone in maternal receptivity receives the presence of the Spirit into the living ground of his or her heart. The person gives birth to wisdom and righteousness, holiness as well as inner purity. And thus everyone can become

[7] Hathaway and Boff, *The Tao of Liberation*, 329–30.

mother of everything according to its essence, as
the Lord himself said.[8]

Christ grows in our innermost and continually transforms us into his own image, into his own beauty,
which then radiates through us into this world.

The question is, what does this image mean? One
can interpret it theologically: When God is born in me,
I come in contact with the unique image that God has
of me. God is also born in me as a child. This means
that God brings me into contact with what's pristine
and genuine in me, with the splendor that God imparts
to every human being at conception. However, God's
birth also means that God permeates all of my spiritual
and bodily faculties and thus becomes more and more
incarnated in me. My task is to allow the divine life to
flow through my thoughts and actions into the world.
To put it another way, the birth of God in my soul opens
my eyes to seeing—even in the secular world—God as
true Reason and to feeling one with the cosmos.

Augustine of Hippo, one of the first mystics in the
West, speaks not of the birth of God in human beings
but of the image of God in us:

We do indeed recognize in ourselves an image
of God, that is, of the Supreme Trinity. It is not
an adequate image but a very distant parallel. It
is not co-eternal; and, in short, it is not of the

---

[8] Hugo Rahner, "Die Gottesgeburt," 375–76.

same substance as God. For all that, there is no
creature in the whole of God's creation so near
to God in its nature; but the image now needs to
be re-fashioned and brought to perfection, so to
become close in resemblance to God.[9]

Thus, the image of God exists in our souls. Here
we recognize our inner kinship with God. Even more,
God's image is reflected on our souls. This gives us
true dignity. Augustine also speaks of the birth of God
in human beings. However, he understands it more
morally and less mystically: "In faith, in the doing of
the good, in the realization of the Father's will, the
soul becomes a bearer of Christ."[10] Meister Eckhart
roots his understanding of God's birth in Augustine's
view, yet he interprets his thought mystically and also
ontologically.

For Meister Eckhart the idea of the birth of God
in the human soul has become central. In the soul's
"spark," as he calls it, the Son is reborn. In it, the Divine appears visible in the soul. Meister Eckhart sees
the birth of God in connection with the Son's birth in
the heart of the Father and the incarnation of God in the
child in Bethlehem. For him, there is no chronological
order. Everything is an expression of the same event,

[9] Augustine, *Concerning the City of God against the Pagans*,
trans. Henry Bettenson, bk. XI, chap. 26 (Baltimore, MD: Penguin
Books, 1972), 459.

[10] Hugo Rahner, "Die Gottesgeburt," 389–90.

which culminates in God's birth in the individual human soul. Meister Eckhart expresses it this way: "God gives birth to His only-begotten Son in you whether you like it or not; whether you are asleep or awake, God does His work."[11]

God effects the birth of God in our souls. For Meister Eckhart, the birth of Jesus from Mary is an expression for what happens in every soul: "It is more worth to God to be born spiritually of the individual virgin or good soul, than that He was physically born of Mary."[12] The birth of God is, however, not only an action of God but also solicits a human response: God "begets His only-begotten Son in the highest part of the soul. In the same moment that He bears His only-begotten Son into me, I bear him back into the Father."[13] For Meister Eckhart, bearing and being born are identical.

Today these bold expressions of the mystic are often quoted in interreligious dialogue. Ultimately, though, we will never be able to understand them entirely. For Meister Eckhart, the birth of God means an intimate relationship between God and the human being.

---

[11] Meister Eckhart, "Sermon Fifty-Three" [On Luke 1:28], in *The Complete Mystical Works of Meister Eckhart*, trans. and ed. Maurice O'C. Walshe, rev. Bernard McGinn, 279–84 (New York: Crossroad Publishing Company, 2009), 282.

[12] Ibid., 279.

[13] Ibid., 281.

# 4.

# The Divine as
# Healing Power in Us

## *The Holy Spirit*

For us Christians, the Divine is always also a healing power. Jesus, the Son of God, heals the sick.[1] In him, God's healing power comes to us. In his inaugural speech at the synagogue of Nazareth, Jesus describes his mission with words from Isaiah: "The Spirit of the Lord is upon me . . . to bring good news to the poor. He has sent me to proclaim release to the captives and recovery of sight to the blind, to let the oppressed go free,

---

[1] Translators' note: In German, Jesus Christ is the bearer of *Heil*, "healing, personal wholeness," which is a manifestation of salvation; Christ is the *Heiland*, the Physician, the Savior.

to proclaim the year of the Lord's favor" (Lk 4:18–19; cf. Isa 61:1). Sent by God, Jesus heals the sick, and he commissions his disciples "to proclaim the kingdom of God and to heal" (Lk 9:2). The proclamation of God's kingdom and the mission of healing go hand in hand. However, as Jesus says in Luke's Gospel (17:21), the kingdom of God is "within you"—"interior in you," as Martin Luther translated it. In other words, the kingdom of God is the inner room of stillness in each of us where God reigns and where we are not dominated by our needs, our neurotic routines, or the expectations and claims of other people. In this room, where the kingdom of God is in us, we are free, we are healed and made whole. There, God's healing power is in us. There, we sense in us the healing power of the Divine.

The Christian tradition links the Divine as healing power with Jesus Christ, the Savior, and also with the Holy Spirit. Jesus is the divine Physician who heals the sick, as recounted in the many healing accounts in the Synoptic Gospels. Jesus heals with God's "power," *dynamis* in Greek. However, Saint John describes Jesus as a physician in the image of the bronze serpent that the Israelites had fixed to a pole so that all people who had been bitten by poisonous snakes would be restored by looking at it. "And just as Moses lifted up the serpent in the wilderness, so must the Son of Man be lifted up, that whoever believes in him may have eternal life" (Jn 3:14–15; cf. Num 21:9). Jesus is the divine Physician who heals our deepest wound, the wound of death [Gen 3:19].

Saint John uses yet another image to clarify that precisely on the cross Jesus becomes our Physician. Jesus says: "And I, when I am lifted up from the earth, will draw all people to myself" (Jn 12:32). On the cross Jesus embraces us, and in this embrace he heals our wounds. In this image the church fathers saw Jesus, on the cross, embracing the whole world. They understood the cross to be the fundamental principle of the world that shapes the whole cosmos. The cross is firmly driven into the world so that it makes steadfast what is unsteady and connects the depths of the earth with the heavens.

In my seminars I sometimes ask the participants to stand up and to extend their arms as Jesus had extended his arms on the cross. In this posture I can imagine that I am embracing the whole cosmos. It is said in Latin, *Nihil humanum mihi alienum* ("Nothing human is alien to me"). Stretching out my arms as on a cross, I can imagine that nothing in the cosmos is alien to me. Everything that exists in the cosmos exists also in me. In this pose I sense my interconnectedness with the whole world.

I often also introduce another exercise in order to illumine the healing effects of the cross. We stand up and cross our arms across our chests. Because Christ embraces us on the cross, we—together with him—embrace the wounded child in us: the abandoned child, the excluded child, the overlooked child, the inadequate child, the bullied child, the misunderstood child, the neglected child, the shamed child, and the rejected child. Then the seminar participants sense something of Jesus's healing power that flows to us from the cross. The cross manifests to us that Jesus's healing love embraces all that is injured, weak, and sick in us.

The church fathers speak of Jesus not only as the Physician who touches us from the outside and heals us. He is also the inner Physician within us, the One who brings us into contact with the healing powers of our souls. God has planted these healing powers into our souls. Through Jesus we come into contact with them. This inner physician speaks words such as: "Stretch out your hand!" (Mk 3:5); or, "Stand up, take your mat, and walk" (Jn 5:8). And he touches our wounds and allows the healing power of God to stream into these wounds so that they are transformed and healed. Paraphrasing the words he spoke to the man with the withered hand and also to the paralyzed man, his healing powers are also at work in us. They are the external words reaching our ears but also the inner words that bring us into contact with the healing power of our souls.

The Divine as healing power exists in us also through the Holy Spirit. Jesus has sent us the Spirit. In John's Gospel he breathes the Holy Spirit into his disciples on Easter evening: "he breathed on them and said to them, 'Receive the Holy Spirit'" (Jn 20:22). The Holy Spirit exists in us like the breath that permeates our being. In the Old Testament, God's Spirit itself is even called God's Breath.[2] In our breath we can sense the Holy Spirit. As much as we cannot live without breathing, we do not live up to our existence as redeemed Christians without the Holy Spirit breathing in and through us. The Spirit is the divine Power that penetrates into all pores of our bodies and our souls. One path to healing is to consciously have this Spirit stream into the sick cells of our bodies. There is no guarantee that they will be healed. But we may be confident that the Holy Spirit's healing power unfolds in our bodies. There will be nothing in us that will not be touched by the Holy Spirit. When we are touched by the Holy Spirit, we come in touch with ourselves, our true selves. Then our illness will not alienate us from ourselves. Rather, it will become the gateway for the Holy Spirit, who will fill us, especially in our infirmity. At the very least our self-perception will be transformed; even in illness, we will no longer feel sick but whole because the Holy Spirit permeates everything in us.

The Pentecost Sequence—"Come, Holy Spirit"—by Stefan Langton extols the Holy Spirit with these words:

---

[2] Translators' note: This allusion to Genesis 1:2 is explicit below; it recognizes that "breath" and "spirit" as well as "wind" are alternative translations of the Hebrew *ruach* in Genesis 1:2.

"Wash clean what is soiled; enliven what is dried up; heal what is tormented by infirmity *(sana quod est saucium)*."

As a prisoner the German Jesuit Alfred Delp—who was arrested in July 1944 because of his resistance to the Third Reich and was executed on February 2, 1945—meditated on the Pentecost Sequence, writing on small pieces of paper to draw consolation and hope for himself from his words. Delp suggests that instead of constantly ruminating about our hurts and making other people responsible for our sufferings, we should simply lift them up to God without continually wondering why this or that has happened to us. He writes:

> At some point all pondering and all thoughts of escape must cease. One must become entirely still, lest the thorns of the brambles into which one has fallen will inflict new wounds. Be entirely still, know your powerlessness, and seek God's healing hand. Weep the tears of His holy and healing stream; let it flow into us, the stream which will strengthen us from within for the task ahead.[3]

According to Delp, in weeping we not only wash out our own misery, but we also open ourselves to the Holy Spirit so that the flood of the Spirit's healing love may gush into us.

---

[3] Alfred Delp, *Gesammelte Schriften*, vol. 4: *Aus dem Gefängnis*, ed. Roman Bleistein (Frankfurt: Josef Knecht, 1984), 292.

Delp speaks not only of the wounds inflicted by others but also of those coming from within ourselves:

> When faith falters, when hope falls apart, when love turns cold, when worship becomes lifeless, when doubt grows, when faint-heartedness covers all of life like the shroud of winter terrain, when hate and arrogance choke one's inner breath, then life is fatally wounded.[4]

Delp knows that human beings cannot heal this wound but must turn to God's Spirit. During his time in prison Delp learned it himself: "On my own, I would have given-in long ago, already back then on Lehrter Street. God heals. God's healing power lives in me and with me."[5]

Alfred Delp's meditations can encourage us to allow the Holy Spirit to heal our wounds. We should not repress our hurts but lift them up to God and envision how God's holy and healing Spirit is flowing into our wounds, is changing and healing them. However, the Holy Spirit heals only what we lift up to God. Therefore, I need to face myself and the hurts of my soul honestly and openly. I myself must see and acknowledge them. Only then I can hold out to God my vulnerability, my powerlessness, my loneliness, my sadness,

---

[4] Ibid., 293.
[5] Ibid.

my anxiety, and my pain so that God's Holy Spirit may flow into all those hurt parts of my soul and body.

Cancer therapy, nowadays, uses the power of imagination. Patients imagine how positive energy is flooding into the cancerous cells and is fighting them. We ourselves can imagine that the Holy Spirit fills our cells and heals them. From quantum physics we know that ideas and images influence the material order. Hence, the divine power of the Holy Spirit can also heal our bodies. However, we must not expect that we can heal each and every illness. Some people think that they may command divine power. When they are not healed, they blame themselves. They think that they didn't believe in it enough. However, it is superstition to think that I myself can "make" faith, to think that I only need to let the healing power enter deeply enough my unconscious and I will be cured. And it is danger-ous. We cannot command the Holy Spirit. We can only beseech the Spirit to enter us and heal all that is sick within us. But how the Holy Spirit manages this we must leave to the Spirit. The Spirit might strengthen us without healing our bodies.

In the liturgy the Holy Spirit is also called the Cre-ator Spirit. The hymn by Rabanus Maurus begins *Veni, Creator Spiritus* ("Come, Creator Spirit"). Through the Holy Spirit, God creates everything. Thus, the Bible states in its creation account that "a wind from God swept over the face of the waters" (Gen 1:2). The Spirit of God permeates the whole world, and this connects everything. This same Spirit connects Christians with the church and us with all of creation, which is permeated by the Spirit. The Creed calls the Spirit *Dominus Vivicans*—the One invigorating us and the whole of creation. Thus, the Holy Spirit is healing by connecting us with the whole creation and filling everything in us with new life. Leonardo Boff speaks of a cosmic-ecological mysticism of the Holy Spirit: "We find ourselves immersed in a field of absolute Energy—the *Spiritus Creator*—who manifests the energies of the universe and in our own vital and spiritual energy."[6]

---

[6] Mark Hathaway and Leonardo Boff, *The Tao of Liberation: Exploring the Ecology of Transformation* (Maryknoll, NY: Orbis Books, 2009), 329.

# 5.

# The Divine That Unifies Us with Ourselves

The Christian tradition understands the one God as the triune God. There are many theological attempts to describe the mystery of this Trinity. The church fathers see a parallel between the triune God and human beings, to whom are ascribed three aspects: body, soul, and spirit, or in the words of Augustine, understanding, will, and memory *(memoria)*. The triune God permeates these three aspects of the human being and unifies them. As the triune God is simply one God, so too the human being, albeit being three aspects, is just one individual. Indeed, the longing of the human being is to become unified. This includes, however, experiencing in one's body unity with the entire cosmos.

Jesus expresses in his farewell discourse, just before his passion, this longing for unity. Praying for his followers, he asks "that they may all be one. As you, Father, are in me and I am in you, may they also be in us. . . . that they may become completely one" (Jn 17:21, 23). Usually, we interpret these words of Jesus in view of the unity of Christians. That is certainly one possible meaning of these words. If, however, we read Jesus's words before the backdrop of Greek philosophy, they also mean something else.

The Greeks were longing for unity. What is the One in all the plurality? What is it that holds everything together? Regarding Heraclitus's philosophy of becoming, Parmenides develops a philosophy of Being, of the One, of the identity that is simultaneously the All. In relation to the One, the many is only an appearance. Plato adopts this philosophy. He sees the unity realized in the *one* idea of the Good. This *one* idea realizes itself in the multitude of visible things. The idea of the One, in Greek *to hen*, becomes central, above all, with Plotinus in Neo-Platonism, which fascinated Augustine. The *hen* is the sign of the Divine. It is the "beyond being." All things emanate from the One.

Now Jesus shows us how we can become one: we are to be one as he and the Father are one. In his incarnation Jesus has drawn everything that is human—even the darkness and the abyss of a human being and horrific death on a cross—into unity with God. Thus, we too become one with ourselves only when we descend, as Jesus did, into the depths of our unconscious. C. G. Jung called these depths the shadow realm. We shall let the light of Jesus illumine all of the shadow aspects of our souls. Also, we have to allow Christ's light to flow into our body and in our body into everything cosmic. Then we become one. Then we no longer exclude anything from this unity. Then, as Jesus says, we will be perfected in unity. The words in Greek are *teteleio-menoi eis to hen*; this phrase literally means "perfected toward the one, into the one." *Teteleiomenoi* is the same word that the evangelist John uses to describe Jesus's love perfected on the cross.[1] Here, he has reconciled all the world's dichotomies: heaven and earth, light and dark, good and evil, male and female, the conscious and the unconscious. John understands Jesus's cross as an embrace; Jesus embraces all of this world in his love. At the same time he embraces us in our dichotomy. This embrace allows us to become one with ourselves. The word *telos* also plays an important role in the Greek mystery cults. It refers to the initiation into the mystery of God and the mystery of the human being.

*Telos* can also mean "wedding." In the story of the wedding feast at Cana, the evangelist John understands the incarnation of God in Jesus as such; that is, in becoming human, God weds us and transforms the stale water in our inner realm into delicious wine [Jn 2:1–12]. This wedding is perfected on the cross. There, Jesus draws darkness and evil, even the brutality of death, into his divine reality; all is permeated with God's love.

---

[1] Translators' note: See John 17:23; 19:28; 19:30; 4:34; 5:36.

The Divine leads to unity in yet another way. When we call to mind that divine Love permeates everything in us, then God is uniting everything in us within God. Then, we can be content with our lives, for there is nothing in us that is not touched by God and infused with God's love. If we allow the experience of the Eucharist to sink deep into our consciousness, we will feel that we are fully and completely penetrated by divine Love. There is nothing anymore in us that would be alien to us, would be estranged or separated from us and from God. All is one with God. This way we can also be one with all that is in us.

Meister Eckhart was fascinated by the notion of the One. In his homily on the virtuous person he writes: "For man must be one in himself and must seek it in himself and in one—that is, to see God alone."[2] In other words, the goal of the human being is to become one with oneself and God. The encounter with God is the prerequisite for a human being to become one with oneself. Hence, Meister Eckhart concludes his homily with a statement that paraphrases the words of a biblical prophet: "In the prophet Hosea, our Lord says, 'I will lead the noble soul into a wilderness, and there I will speak into her heart' (Hos 2:14), one with One, one from One, one in One, and a single One

---

[2] Meister Eckhart, "The Nobleman," in *The Complete Mystical Works of Meister Eckhart*, trans. and ed. Maurice O'C. Walshe, rev. Bernard McGinn, 557–65 (New York: Crossroad Publishing Company, 2009), 564. Translators' note: The German title of Eckhart's homily is *der edele Mensch*, "the virtuous person."

eternally. Amen."[3] In sum, God wants to make us one with ourselves and to empower us to become one with the One—with the one God who in Godself is the highest unity and who enables us to become one with ourselves. However, this becoming one with God and in ourselves is only possible if we let go of ourselves, if we let go of all agendas, let go of all images that we have made of ourselves and God—in other words, when we live "detached" or "serene" lives. Concerning this detachment Meister Eckhart writes:

> This immovable detachment brings a man into the greatest likeness to God. For the reason why God is God is because of his immovable detachment, and from this detachment He has His purity, His simplicity, and His immutability. Therefore, if a man is to be like God, as far as a creature can have a likeness with God, this must come from detachment.[4]

I would like to bring this insight of God unifying everything within me and leading me into unity into my daily life. All of us know the feeling of loneliness. We feel abandoned, isolated from others. No one has time for us. There is no one with whom we can speak. Even when there are people around us, we may still feel

---

[3] Ibid.

[4] Meister Eckhart, "On Detachment," in *The Complete Works of Meister Eckhart*, 569.

alone because they do not understand us. At this point the creative challenge is to transform this loneliness into a sense of all-being-one. But how can I do this?

I sit down and come in touch with my sadness about my being alone, about my loneliness. I pass through the sad feelings and reach the bottom of my soul. Now, I call to mind that I am one with all human beings. In the depths of my soul I am connected with all who—like myself—are suffering in their loneliness. This transforms my sad feeling of aloneness into a oneness with all human beings. I imagine how in the depths of my soul I am united with the entire creation. When I am sitting on a bench, surrounded by a beautiful land-scape, I can imagine that I am one with all of nature around me. Everything that is in nature is also in me. I feel lifted up and whole. I imagine that I am one with God at the Source of my soul. In God, I am one with myself. There I can say yes to myself, approve of me as I am. It is a healing experience to know myself as whole. I do not feel isolated anymore but connected with everything, belonging to all human beings and to all that is. This experience transforms my sadness into a deep inner peace.

# 6.

# The Divine as the Room of Stillness in Us

Evagrius Ponticus, one of the desert fathers, speaks of the inner room of stillness in each of us. Evagrius names it "God's Place"—the place where God dwells in us. For Evagrius, this is a room where all human thoughts and images of God are silent and where the noise of one's own thoughts cease. It is a room beyond all words and images. Evagrius exhorts those who pray: "The spirit that possesses health is the one which has no images of the things of this world at the time of prayer."[1] The room of stillness is, at the same time, the room of wordless and non-pictorial

---

[1] Evagrius Ponticus, *The Praktikos Chapters on Prayer*, trans. John Eudes Bamberger, OCSO (Spencer, MA: Cistercian Publications, 1970), #65, 34.

prayer. God is experienced as the Mystery beyond all concepts and images.

The mystics have described this inner room of stillness in various images. Meister Eckhart speaks of the soul's "spark." Johannes Tauler speaks of the "ground of the soul." Catherine of Siena names this room of stillness "the inner cell."

Teresa of Avila used the image of "the interior castle." The interior castle has different rooms. Passing through all these rooms, I reach the innermost chamber. There, only God lives with me. I can also imagine this interior room as a grotto, a cave. Icons have always depicted the birth of Jesus in a grotto. The grotto is a maternal room. It represents as well the center of the cosmos. My interior room of stillness is, as it were, the grotto God has carved into the cosmos in order to dwell in me and the entire creation; there, God, the innermost reality, holds everything together.

The Christian tradition draws a connection between the image of the interior room of silence and the biblical story of a squall on the Sea of Galilee. The disciples are in the boat and are being tossed back and forth by a great windstorm. They are afraid. Jesus, however, is not bothered by the storm. He sleeps peacefully on a cushion [Mk 4:35–41].

The boat is a metaphor for us. Our boat is being tossed around by a windstorm. Water is spilling into the boat. But where Jesus is in our boat there is peace. The storm does not trouble him. Like us, the disciples are afraid of the storm. Therefore, they wake Jesus. "He woke up and rebuked the wind, and said to the sea, 'Peace! Be still!' Then the wind ceased, and there was a dead calm" (Mk 4:39). In the Greek text it reads *galena megale*: there was a "great stillness." Jesus calms the world around us. The elements of the world—the storms and waves—die down. From Jesus emanates a calming effect, reaching even into the cosmos. When the cosmos becomes still around us, we can experience in our hearts the great stillness or silence that Jesus creates in us when he rebukes the storms of our emotions. He calms the inner noise of our thoughts. But this means that we have to wake him; we have to build a relationship with him. As long as he sleeps, as long as we have no relationship to the One who is in the inner room of stillness, we do not share in his peace, in his stillness. There, where Jesus dwells in us and where we are in relationship with him, there exists a great stillness in us, for the noise from the outside no longer has access.

In this room of stillness we experience ourselves in five different modes.

1. We are free from the noise of human thoughts, from the demands and claims of other people, from their expectations and their judgments. Many people are concerned about what others will say, whatever they do. However, the opinions of others do not intrude into this inner room of stillness.

2. We are healed and made whole. Harmful words cannot reach into this inner room of stillness.

They will still offend us emotionally. However, this interior room of stillness is free from all that is hurtful. It is a place of refuge where we find rescue from the hurts and illnesses that affect us from the outside.

3. In this room we are original and authentic. There, all of the images others have imposed on us dissipate: the images of little self-worth that belittle us and tell us that we are obnoxious, that no one can put up with us. In this place any form of hubris dissipates; we're free from the feeling that we must always be perfect and successful and "with it." When all of these images dissolve, then we are simply present. We are pure being and participate in the pure being of God. We are free from the need of having to justify ourselves or to prove ourselves. Today many people are first and foremost ready to ask, "What's in it for me?" When I am simply present, there is nothing to gain. I experience what Angelus Silesius expressed this way:

The rose is without why, it blooms
because it blooms,
It pays no attention to itself, asks not
whether it is seen.[2]

---

[2] Angelus Silesius, "Without Why," in *The Cherubinic Wanderer*, trans. Maria Shrady (New York: Paulist Press, 1986), Book I, #289, 54.

4. In this room we are pure and clear. The self-reproaches and the feelings of guilt have no access here, and we come in touch with the pure, unspotted, and unclouded image of God in us. Many people do not settle down, either because they are afraid of missing out on things or because feelings of guilt suddenly emerge. However, there—where Christ dwells in us—we are without guilt. There, everything is wonderful and good as it was at the beginning of creation.

5. There, where the mystery of God dwells in us, we are at home with ourselves. There, we find ourselves, and we are comfortable in our own presence.

When I am in the bustle of a large city, it is helpful to remind myself that there is this inner room of stillness. Despite the noise surrounding me, I feel at peace with myself. I remain with myself, and I imagine that none of the rushing activity around me concerns me. I acknowledge it, but there is this room of silence within me to which the noise from the outside has no access. When I served as the business manager for our monastic community, I had to chair meetings. Sometimes we had heated discussions over different opinions. At these moments I found it helpful to focus my thoughts on that room of stillness at the bottom of my soul. Then I could enter into these conversations without becoming upset, because the center of my soul remained untouched; it remained still.

In seminars and at our retreat center I offer spiritual counseling. Some people ask me how I can keep going as I listen to so much suffering and so many problems. Again, my answer is this: I open myself with empathy to the other person. At the same time, however, I am aware of the inner room into which no one has access. This relieves me from the burden during the conversations. I have an interior shelter where I can always find refuge when I am emotionally too much engaged. I surely empathize with the other, but I also relativize the feelings by going deeper into myself and enter into the inner room of stillness at the bottom of my soul. There God dwells in me. To this God I can entrust all of the problems I hear about. I do not have to solve everything on my own.

That God can be experienced only in the silence is the message of the well-known story of the prophet Elijah [1 Kgs 19:1–21]. Until he had the experience that the Bible's account recalls, he had thought that God answers only in glaring ways such as storms, fire, or earthquakes. However, God taught Elijah a lesson and came to him in the gentle stirring of a breeze, in the "voice of lingering silence," as Martin Buber translated 1 Kings 19:12.[3] Stillness is needed to experience God. The noise of our thoughts separates us from God. However, we must silence not only the noise. As long as we are pondering about God, we are not one with God. We must let go of our thoughts so that we may become one with God.

---

[3] In the NRSV, "after the fire a sound of sheer silence."

# 7.

# The Divine as Love

The First Letter of John states: "God is love, and those who abide in love abide in God, and God abides in them" (1 Jn 4:16). This is a courageous definition: God is love. The love of which John writes is more than a sentiment. It is a quality of being. The expression is to be understood reciprocally: God—in God's essence—is love. However, everywhere we experience love, we are living in God and participating in God. For John, God is both; God is love in God's self, and yet God is also the personal mystery whom we love and who loves us. God expresses divine love for us in sending us the Son. Thus, it says in John 3:16, "For God so loved the world that he gave his only Son, so that everyone who believes in him may not perish but may have eternal life." God shows us eternal love in the Son. Here, God's love lights up for us. When we believe in this love, which precisely shines forth in full glory in the death of God's Son, then we have eternal life; we will experience already here a life that can no longer be destroyed by death. Our consciousness will be transformed and expanded already here. We shall experience what we have known since Jesus's resurrection: love is stronger than death.

Besides these personal words about love, John says still more: God is love, and we experience God when we experience love in us. Each one of us desires to love and to be loved. Each of us has experiences of fulfillment and disappointment, of enchantment and hurt. The goal of our longing is not that someone loves us so that we are "satisfied" forever. Rather, the goal is that we not only love and are loved, but that we ourselves become love. This is what John means with his statement. However, what does it mean to become love? A woman has told me: "Once, when I was meditating, I was suddenly love itself. I did not think specifically about someone. I was simply love. Love flowed through me into my room and to my family, my cat, and the natural world outside. I felt connected with everything, the entire cosmos. I felt one with everything." This woman experienced what John intended to convey: when we are love, then we are connected with everything; we are one with the whole world. A reconciling and unifying energy will emanate from us, an energy in which we experience God's love as a quality of our own human existence.

This experience is described further in John's Gospel: Jesus exhorts: "Abide in my love" (Jn 15:9). Here, John uses the word *agape*. Agape is divine love. It is, as it were, a room in which we can dwell, abide, and live. However, this love also ought to be shown in our love for one another.

Love involves upholding Jesus's commands. This does not sound very inviting. However, it means that love should show itself in a certain attitude toward other people, that love needs an order, a discipline.

Moreover, to love means to interact respectfully with the world, people, and all things. Jesus's command is never interpreted as a concrete directive. Rather, it is in line with his attitude and conduct. He himself said, "No one has greater love than this, to lay down one's life for one's friends" (Jn 15:13). Jesus's love shows itself in his commitment to his friends, and it culminates on the cross.

Saint Paul sings his Great Hymn of Love in 1 Corinthians (chap. 13). This text is often read at weddings. It does not specifically speak, however, only of the love between a man and a woman, or of love for neighbors, or even love for God. We can understand the text only when we read it in the context of Greek philosophy. Similar to the Greeks, Paul speaks of the power of love. From his Christian perspective he interprets this power to be the love that is the gift of the Holy Spirit. This love of God is poured into our hearts through the Holy Spirit (cf. Rom 5:5). Paul calls love a charism, a gift, both an ability of a human being and a gift of God to a human being. It is love that transforms a human being into a person in the first place. It causes in us everything that is beneficial for us: "Love is patient; love is kind; love is not envious or boastful or arrogant" (1 Cor 13:4). Paul is not presenting moral demands. Rather, he intends to describe the effects of this love, this force given as a gift to a human being. Love is a revolutionary force. This becomes clear when Paul writes that love "bears all things, believes all things, hopes all things, endures all things" (1 Cor 13:7). Love is the force that sustains the transforming process of a revolution. It continues to trust, despite all setbacks; it hopes for a better life; and it defies whatever stands in the way of this transformation.

Whether he was conscious of it or not, Paul was writing in dialogue with the philosophy of that time. Paul was educated not only in Jewish theology but also in Greek philosophy. His letters lead to the conclusion that he was well acquainted with Stoic philosophy. And he wanted Christians as they undergo transformation to surpass in their conduct the ethical demands of Stoic thought. Thus, he writes to the Philippians, a community of Greek Christians: "Whatever is true, whatever is honorable, whatever is just, whatever is pure, whatever is pleasing, whatever is commendable, if there is any excellence and if there is anything worthy of praise, think about these things" (Phil 4:8). This statement is a summary of what the Stoic philosophers expected from their disciples. However, in his Great Hymn of Love, Paul refers not so much to the ethical aspects. Rather, similar to Greek philosophers, he describes love as a power in its own right, as a source out of which human beings are creative, as a force that empowers them.

Paul's text about love reflects the philosophical texts of that time about the mystery of love. For example, Plato—most likely the greatest Greek philosopher—sings of love as a power that can do a great deal in a human being:

> Thus I conceive, Phaedrus, that Love [*Eros*] was originally of surpassing beauty and good, and is latterly the cause of similar excellences in others. And now I am moved to summon the aid of verse, and tell how it is he who makes—
>> Peace among men and a windless waveless main;
>> Repose for winds, and slumber in our pain.
>> He it is who casts alienation out, draws intimacy in.[1]

A text by Maximus of Tyre, a rhetorician and philosopher, is even closer to Paul's Great Hymn. Maximus writes:

---

[1] These sentences from Plato's *Symposium* (197c–197e) are discussed in relation to 1 Corinthians 13:1–13 in Hans Conzelmann, *1 Corinthians: A Commentary on the First Epistle to the Corinthians*, trans. James W. Leitch (Philadelphia: Fortress Press, 1975), 219.

But nothing is so hostile to love [*eros*] as necessity. For love is a thing superb and free in extreme, and even more free than Sparta herself. For love alone of everything pertaining to men when it subsists with purity, neither admires wealth, nor dreads a tyrant, nor is astonished by an empire, nor avoids a court of judicature, nor flees from death. It does not consider as dire either wild beasts, or fire, or a precipice, or the sea, or a sword, or a halter; but to it things impervious are most pervious, things dire are most easily vanquished, things terrible are most readily encountered, and things difficult are most speedily accomplished. . . . It is everywhere confident, despises all things, and subdues all things.[2]

In both texts love is understood as God's gift that shapes the life of a human being and gives it a new "flavor." Those who are filled with love are not affected by life's turbulence. They lose the feeling of inner estrangement. They come into contact with themselves. They remain centered. Plato uses images when he speaks of love: love bestows peace among people and, amid this world's turbulence, brings us into contact with the inner room of stillness. Love opens a room in our hearts in which we find serenity. It brings us in touch with our true being, creates intimacy with

---

[2] These sentences from Maximus of Tyre's *Dissertations*, 1:103, are discussed in relation to 1 Corinthians 13:1–13 in Conzelmann, *1 Corinthians*, 220.

ourselves, that is, with the inner and original image of what God has intended for us.

For Maximus of Tyre love is a force and power that nothing in the world can resist. Although love is not armed, tyrants fear it. This theme repeatedly surfaces among Greek writers. In *The Odes of Anacreon* the poet sings: "Neither cavalry nor infantry nor the marines have destroyed me. No, I was defeated by a different, new power that alone can strike down with a glance."[3] Love finds a way to the other person who otherwise would be closed. Love is, therefore, a revolutionary energy that is stronger than the weapons of war. It can end wars. The texts of the Greek philosophers hoped to communicate this confidence in the revolutionary energy of love in much the same way as Saint Paul's Great Hymn of Love. The close resemblance between the texts of Paul and Maximus becomes clear as each concludes with words in praise of love: Maximus ends his text with a threefold "everything." Paul picks up this theme and ends his Hymn of Love with similar words: Love "bears all things, believes all things, hopes all things, endures all things" (1 Cor 13:7).

Plato expresses his thoughts on love in the words of three guests whom he invited to a dinner symposium.[4]

---

[3] See Anacreon, "Ode 26," in *The Odes of Anacreon*, trans. Thomas Moore (London: John Stockdale, 1800), 107–8.

[4] See Plato, *Symposium*, trans. Michael Joyce, in *The Collected Dialogues of Plato, including the Letters*, ed. Edith Hamilton and Huntington Cairns, 526–74 (Princeton, NJ: Princeton University Press, 1971).

The first one is Eryximachus. He regards *Eros* as a cosmic energy. The Greek word for love, *eros*, pertains not only to the love between a man and a woman but is to be understood as a force that permeates the entire living world or, in the nonliving natural world, that evokes harmony in everything. Love is the law of existence. It brings everything together and wants to harmonize all of life's dichotomies, both in the living and also in the nonliving natural world. This understanding of love is important for a spirituality of ecology; love is the power that pervades the entire cosmos. It creates interconnectedness in the world. Today's theory of evolution is no longer based on the presupposition of the survival of the fittest, as Darwin postulated. Rather, it assumes that organisms have survived because they have felt interconnected. Love is, therefore, the driving force of evolution. Boff speaks of this cosmic love when he asserts that "love is the great, unifying, and integrative force of the universe."[5] It connects us as well with the entire cosmos.

Aristophanes, an ancient poet and another guest at Plato's dinner, recognizes love as the essential structure of the existence of the human being. He recounts the myth that, in the beginning, man and woman were spherical, forming together one existence. As Zeus was afraid that these superior human beings could become

---

[5] Mark Hathaway and Leonardo Boff, *The Tao of Liberation: Exploring the Ecology of Transformation* (Maryknoll, NY: Orbis Books, 2009), 333.

a threat to the gods, he cut the two apart. The result of this act was *Eros,* who emerged as the longing of each one for the original other half. Plato interprets this myth to mean that love in its origins belongs to human beings. "When people encounter their original half in the good fortune of love, they encounter their own selves and affirm them."[6] Hence, love leads human beings to their true selves.

Plato expresses his own thoughts about *Eros* in the speech he puts on the lips of his teacher Socrates. For Socrates, *Eros* is not a god but an intermediate being between God and human beings. *Eros* wants to bring human beings in contact with the good. It is the force that generates beauty. In *Eros,* human beings bear a generative power in themselves—in their bodies as well as their souls. The generative power of the body unites with the body of the woman and that way creates new life, whereby a mortal human shares in the immortal.

The soul, too, generates knowledge and spiritual-intellectual values. Poets, artists, and philosophers are no longer concerned only about observing the beauty of an individual body but also about perceiving beauty in itself. Love ascends from actual, beautiful bodies

---

[6] Johannes Hirschberger, "Der platonische Eros," in *Was heisst Liebe? Zur Tradition eines Begriffes*, Rabanus Maurus Akademie, 30–46 (Frankfurt: Knecht, 1982), 34.

to primordial beauty, which is the basis of all things. The greatest bliss for the human being is to behold primordial beauty.

Socrates's speech makes an important connection between love and beauty. The German word *schön* ("beautiful") has its roots in the German verb *schauen* ("to behold"). When I behold myself with love, I am beautiful. Also, when I behold another human being with love, I find this individual to be beautiful. Only a human being who hates or disdains himself or herself is ugly. Whoever hates others makes them ugly. The Russian writer Dostoevsky asserts: "Beauty will save the world."[7] In beholding the beauty of the world with love, we approach it with gentle care. Then, we look after the world. The word *schön* originates not only from *schauen* but also from *schonen* ("to care for"). Love leads to a caring relation with the world and, precisely in this relationship, recognizes its beauty.

Plato understands *Eros* as the powerful energy that connects what is separated. *Eros* is the desire for unification. For us, it is also the essence of love; it unites what is divided. It brings together the diverging forces of the cosmos, and it unites human beings. Pierre Teilhard de Chardin, the French Jesuit and philosopher, has translated this view of love for our contemporary world. He speaks of "amorization."[8] The entire world, even

---

[7] Fyodor Dostoevsky, *The Idiot*, trans. Constance Garnett (New York: Bantam Books, 1981), 370.

[8] See Pierre Teilhard de Chardin, *The Heart of Matter*, trans. René Hague (New York: Harcourt Brace Jovanovich, 1976), 39–57.

what's nonliving, is permeated by the love of Christ. For Teilhard, the opening in the side of Jesus on the cross symbolizes the moment when divine love flows out of Christ's heart for all people and into the whole cosmos and permeates everything with love [Jn 19:34]. Thus, today we encounter the love of Jesus everywhere, in people and the natural world.

The church fathers further developed the thoughts of Paul and Plato on love. Some modern exegetes, primarily Lutheran, perceive *agape* as the pure love of God, in juxtaposition to *eros* as love motivated by personal lust. Nevertheless, the church fathers wished to overcome this kind of antithesis. In describing God's love for us, they speak not only of God's *agape* (*caritas* or *dilectio*, in Latin) but also of *eros* (*amor*, in Latin) as a characteristic of God's love for human beings. Origen recasts John's definition "God is *agape*" into "God is *eros*." God loves human beings passionately. Also, our love of God ought to show the passionate fervor of *Eros*.

For me, these reflections mirror not only the history of theology, but in them I also see the attempt to unite the gift of God's love—which works in us through the Holy Spirit—with natural love and the energy of *eros*. Without *eros*, our love becomes lackluster. Without *eros*, our love would not have the power to unite what is separated. The passion of *eros* is needed to overcome the political and societal divisions in our world. The passion of *eros* is needed so that we treat creation with tender care and lead it into a good future. Love is not only something gentle and placid; it is rather the passionate yearning for union and healing, as Greek mythology understood *Eros*.

For Plato, love is a divine force that pervades the entire existence of the world. It prevents the world from disintegrating, reuniting over and over again that which was separated. In our time, Gabriel Marcel has picked up this idea of Plato. For this French philosopher love is identical with being. Love is the primal ground of all being. Hence, it is present in everything. Love is also the foundation of human existence. This means not only "that everyone receives everything from love but also that everything that a human being is and has is only fully possessed in love, while without love everything slips away and, in the end, a human being stands before nothing."[9]

Gabriel Marcel understands love to be the foundational reality of our existence. Without love we do not find our true selves. We attain that which God has given us only in love. Whether it is love in marriage or in friendship, or the love of God for us or our love for God—in all of these, we experience in some way love as being, as existence itself; love heals and perfects everything. Gabriel Marcel knows the difference between being and having, the difference that Erich Fromm presented later in his book *The Art of Loving*. Whoever realizes being or existence itself also participates

---

[9] Johannes B. Lotz, "Die Liebe als Herausforderung des Menschen," in *Was heisst Liebe?*, 9–29 at 24.

in love, for being and loving are one. I cannot simply "have" love as a possession. Rather, it is a matter of *being* love and experiencing a new existence through love. Whoever opens to another human being in love shares in the Absolute Being as love. This person "experiences existence in the presence of the light, in the fullness of being."[10]

In their mutual presence human beings who love one another touch on the eternal. Love is the power that overcomes death; it is stronger than death. For Gabriel Marcel love means to say to one's beloved: "You, you shall not die." Even in death we will not cease to love and to be loved. On the contrary, in death we will experience love in its pure form, in its pure existence.

When, during my meditations, I enter into the room of stillness within me, I always sense that this room is filled with love. Once I spoke with a Buddhist nun who is a Zen master about my experiences during meditation. I said that I meditate with the Jesus Prayer, which leads me into the room of stillness beyond all words. For me, this room of stillness is a room of love. At this, she noted that, for her, love would be too exhausting. For her, it would be a room of emptiness. I replied that, for me, emptiness is too cold. As we continued, it became evident that when she heard the word *love,* she immediately thought of the emotional and erotic love

[10] Georg Scherer, "Die Liebe im Denken Gabriel Marcels," in *Was heisst Liebe?*, 112–33 at 130.

between a man and a woman. For me, love is rather a quality of existence, the Reason of all being. For Buddhists, on the other hand, emptiness is not cold but filled with compassion. It is solely void of thoughts, deliberations, and emotions. Before we begin to moralize about the need to love one another, we should begin by entering into the inner space of stillness where the Source of love wells up within us. It is a room full of love that—at the bottom of our soul—connects us with the love that permeates all of creation.

# 8.

# Transparency

## *Transcendence and Immanence*

God transcends all finite reality, surpassing everything that we apprehend here with our senses.
Nevertheless, if we speak only of God's transcendence
without also stressing God's immanence, then our faith
becomes an escape from the world. On the one hand,
God is the transcendent God who surpasses all that is
visible and experiential. On the other hand, God is present in all things; we may find God in everything that is.

Whatever is true of God is also true of human beings. If we wish to experience God, we must transcend
the world. We must leave behind us everything that is
visible in order to behold what is invisible. But, at the
same time, we experience God as the foundation of all

being. God is present in everything, permeates everything. The author of the Acts of the Apostles has expressed this view in the words of Paul's widely known speech at the Areopagus, words the Greek philosophers could also understand: "For 'In him we live and move and have our being'; as even some of your own poets have said, 'For we too are his offspring'" (Acts 17:28). God is present in everything, and we move in God because God's presence enfolds us in everything that surrounds us.

Augustine was constantly drawn to the question of God's transcendence. Guided by Neo-Platonism, he separated the visible, changing world of appearances from the realm of ideas, which is the source of the world of appearances and yet surpasses it. Augustine continually ponders the tension between transcendence and history. For him, the transcendent God is also the God who informs history. Thereby, Augustine moves from external transcendence to inner transcendence. The spirit of the human being has not only a relationship to the Absolute that surpasses all earthly reality, but it also returns to itself, to the bottom of its soul. Augustine calls this inward movement the "transcending" of the soul to its own foundation. In this regard God is closer to the soul than the soul is to itself. Thus, Augustine states: "Do not go outside, come back to yourself. It is in the inner self that the Truth dwells."[1]

---

[1] Augustine, "True Religion (*De vera religione*)," trans. Edmund Hill, OP, in *On Christian Belief*, ed. Boniface Ramsey, in *The Works*

God dwells in this truth. In his *Confessions*, Augustine addresses God: "Yet you were deeper than my inmost understanding and higher than the topmost height that could reach."[2] The entire striving of Augustine consists in going beyond everything visible, even beyond one's own feelings and thoughts, in order to enter into that inner room in which God dwells. Nevertheless, he says that this inner room is not a place. We can only call it as such. God dwells in no place; God exists without a place. In his *Confessions* Augustine asks God:

> Where, then, did I find you so that I could learn of you? For you were not in my memory before I learned of you. Where else, then, did I find you, to learn of you, unless it was in yourself, above me? Whether we approach you or depart from you, you are not confined in any place. You are Truth, and you are everywhere present where all seek counsel of you.[3]

All of these thoughts on the transcendence of God may seem to us to be an escape from the world. However, the opposite is true: Augustine finds God in the beauty

---

*of Saint Augustine*, Part I, vol. 8, ed. John E. Rotelle, OSA, 29–104 (New Hyde Park, NY: New City Press, 2005), 78.

[2] Augustine, *Confessions*, trans. R. S. Pine-Coffin (Baltimore: Penguin Books, 1961), Book III, #6, 62.

[3] Ibid., Book X, #26, 231.

of the world. God's beauty has poured itself into the world. Thus, Augustine beholds it with eyes of faith and, consequently, recognizes God in everything. God dwells within all things; *Deus interior omni re.*[4] Yet, all things point beyond themselves to the God who exists beyond all things. In his *Confessions* Augustine describes this transcending movement of the world toward its inner beauty:

> Suppose, we said, that the tumult of a man's flesh were to cease and all that his thoughts can conceive, of earth, of water, and or air, should no longer speak to him; suppose that the heavens and even his own soul were silent, no longer thinking of itself but passing beyond; suppose that his dreams and the visions of his imagination spoke no more and that every tongue and every sign and all that is transient grew silent—for all these things have the same message to tell, if only we can hear it, and their message is this: we did not make ourselves, but he who abides forever made us.[5]

For Augustine, God is the challenge to transcend oneself and the world and, at the same time, to enter deeply into the world and one's inner being in order to recognize God—in the innermost reality of the soul and

---

[4] See Augustine, *On Genesis (De Genesi ad litteram)*, trans. Edmund Hill, OP, in Rotelle, *The Works of Saint Augustine*, Part I, vol. 13, Book VIII, 26.48, 374.

[5] Augustine, *Confessions*, Book IX, #10, 198.

in all things in this world—as the One who alone can fulfill our deepest longing. Our longing is kindled by the beauty of the world in all of its facets. However, it reaches beyond the world. By being in touch with this longing, we are also in touch with our souls. Thus, human beings in their essence live in the world and fully participate in it, and simultaneously, in their longing they transcend it toward God and toward the innermost of the Spirit in whom God dwells in them—closer to themselves than they are to themselves.

Although Augustine's thoughts on transcendence fascinate me, I would nevertheless stress nowadays God's immanence. God exists in everything that is: in matter, the plants, the animals, and human beings. God is the Reason of all being. Theology calls this panentheism. Panentheism is distinct from pantheism.[6] Pantheism claims that everything is identical with God. In contrast, panentheism does not identify the natural world with God but believes that God exists in everything—and yet is distinct from everything.

If I were to give an answer to Augustine, I would not say that my life's most important goal is to transcend this world. Rather, I want to become transparent for the

---

[6] Translators' note: The word *panentheism* comes from the Greek *pan-en-theos* ("everything in God"). *Pantheism* comes from the Greek, *pan-theos* ("everything [is] God"). See below, Chapter 18.

Spirit of Jesus. I want Jesus's love to radiate through my words, through my actions, and, yes, through my entire body. For me, Jesus's words about the eye being a light has become an image for this kind of transparency:

> Your eye is the lamp of your body. If your eye is healthy ["healthy," *haplous* in Greek, means "indivisible," "simple"], your whole body is full of light; but if it is not healthy" ["not healthy," *poneros* in Greek, means "wicked"], your body is full of darkness. Therefore, consider whether the light in you is not darkness. If then your whole body is full of light, with no part of it in darkness, it will be as full of light as when a lamp gives you light with its rays. (Lk 11:34–36)

My eyes will show whether I am transparent for the Spirit of Jesus, for his light, for his love. If they radiate light, love, goodness, and mercy, then Jesus's love radiates through them into the world. I will transform this world through Jesus's love, which radiates through my body to my surroundings—not only to human beings but also to the natural world that enfolds me.

Thomas of Celano, a Franciscan chronicler of the thirteenth century, observed the influence of the love that went out from Saint Francis of Assisi into the natural world: "He had such deep love for creatures that even those without reason could recognize his affection and sense his loving kindness."[7] This account resonates with the experience of Fidelis Ruppert, our former abbot, when he withdrew for a few days into the primeval forests of Peru. As he told the story:

> When I am at peace with myself, when Jesus's love lights up within me and radiates out from me, then I am at peace with creation; then the wild animals pose no threats. The legend of the wolf at Gubbio, which peacefully followed after Francis, can indeed be true. Animals sense when someone radiates something of the Spirit of Jesus. In those moments there unfolds the unity between the cosmos and human beings.

Not only human beings but also the entire cosmos are transparent for God. Pierre Teilhard de Chardin speaks the transparency of the cosmos for divine love and coins the term *diaphany* for God's "shining through" in the universe.[8] God's love shines through everything, through matter and through plants, animals,

---

[7] Thomas of Celano's statement is quoted here from Mark Hathaway and Leonardo Boff, *The Tao of Liberation: Exploring the Ecology of Transformation* (Maryknoll, NY: Orbis Books, 2009), 334. See Thomas of Celano, *Thomas of Celano's First Life of Saint Francis of Assisi*, trans. Christopher Stace (London: Society for Promoting Christian Knowledge, 2000), chap. 21, #59.

[8] Translators' note: The term *diaphany* comes from the Greek *dia* ("through") and *phanein* ("to appear, to manifest").

and human beings. Teilhard stands for a cosmic mysticism that begins as

> crimson gleams of Matter, gliding imperceptibly into the gold of Spirit, ultimately to become transformed into the incandescence of a Universe that is Person—and through all this there blows, animating it and spreading over it a fragrant balm, a zephyr of Union—and of the Feminine.
>
> The Diaphany of the Divine at the heart of a glowing Universe, as I have experienced it through contact with the Earth—the Divine radiating from the depths of blazing Matter.[9]

During his youth Teilhard was influenced by his mother's devotion to the Sacred Heart of Jesus. Later, he transformed this devotion as he related it to the cosmos. Already for the young Teilhard, the heart of Jesus was the fire that "had become able to insinuate itself everywhere, to be metamorphosed into no matter what; and so, in as much as it was patient of being universalized, it could in [the] future force its way into, and so amoritize, the cosmic Milieu."[10] He speaks of the entire cosmos as being permeated by and transparent to Christ's love. However, he also speaks of the love with which we should love the cosmos. The love we have for

---

[9] Pierre Teilhard de Chardin, *The Heart of Matter*, trans. René Hague (New York: Harcourt Brace Jovanovich, 1976), 16.
[10] Ibid., 44.

the cosmos transforms it even more into Christ, becoming "a new Charity in which all the Earth's dynamic passions combine as they are divinized."[11]

Teilhard replaces the biblical notion of epiphany—the earthly manifestation of God's glory in Jesus Christ—with the notion of diaphany; that is, the entire world is permeated by the love of Christ. Thus, mysticism is nothing other than to behold the world with different eyes. Evagrius Ponticus already had written of the *theoria physike*, of the "contemplation of the world." One form of mysticism among the first monks was that they meditated on the world in a way that recognized God in everything. Evagrius speaks of the *gnosis ton onton alethes*, which can be translated as the "beholding of the essence of all things." I behold the cosmos in such a way that it may become transparent for its primordial foundation, for God, for the love that—according to Teilhard—is the essence of God.

---

[11] Ibid., 53.

# 9.

# Final Thoughts

## *Love, the Source and Reason of the Whole Creation*

My spirituality focuses above all on the individual human being. It is a mystical spirituality that culminates in the understanding that God dwells in us, is born in us, and that there is in each of us a room of stillness in which the kingdom of God is in us, in which God reigns. Through the encounter with the writings of Leonardo Boff, though, it has become clear to me that I must expand my view. In my writings I have always shared my love for nature, which I treat with care. I am cultivating a spiritual relationship with it by marveling at God's beauty in nature, stepping back in awe. Beauty has become for me an important hint of God. In the beauty of creation, I behold God.

Nevertheless, it has now become clear to me that I must understand myself not only as an "other" in relation to the natural world but as a human being who, in one's essence, is one with the cosmos. Everything that happens in me has an impact on the cosmos. Today we cannot talk about spirituality without also considering our intrinsic unity with the cosmos.

I hope, therefore, that my thoughts—which focus on the indwelling of God in every human person—are open to Leonardo Boff's perspective on the diaphany of the cosmos, on the shining of God's beauty and love through everything that exists. When I discover God, who dwells in me, at the bottom of my soul, I always feel at one with the Reason of all existence, with the cosmos. In unity with God I always experience the God who, as Love, is the Wellspring and Reason of the entire cosmos.

Part Two

# The Divine in Us
# and the Universe

LEONARDO BOFF

**Leonardo Boff**

LEONARDO BOFF is a Brazilian theologian and philosopher who serves as Professor Emeritus of Ethics, Philosophy of Religion, and Ecology at Rio de Janeiro State University. Born in 1938, he entered the Franciscan order in 1959 and was ordained in 1964. After studies in Munich, he received his doctorate in theology and philosophy in 1970. Boff became widely known for his role in developing the theology of liberation, publishing influential works on Christology, ecclesiology, and other themes. In 1985, following the publication of his work *Church: Charism and Power,* he was directed by Cardinal Joseph Ratzinger (later Pope Benedict XVI), prefect of the Congregation of Doctrine of the Faith, to spend a year in silence. When this penalty was later renewed, Boff chose to leave the Franciscan order and priestly ministry. As he commented, "I changed trenches to continue the same fight." In 2001, he was honored with the Right Livelihood Award, sometimes called the alternative Nobel prize, in Stockholm, Sweden.

In light of his eightieth birthday (preparing to "descend the mountain of life"), Boff offered these thoughts about the various passions that have motivated his work.

- The first passion was for the church renewal that began at the Second Vatican Council.
- The second passion was for the historical Jesus and the witness that led to the cross.
- The third passion was for Saint Francis of Assisi, the first following the last (Jesus).

- The fourth passion was for the poor and op-
  pressed; so was born the theology of liberation.
- The fifth passion was for our super-exploited
  Mother Earth.
- The sixth passion was for the human condition,
  in both its wisdom and dementia.
- The seventh passion was for the life of the Spirit.

He writes: "I have published nearly one hundred
books. When people ask me: 'What are you doing in
life?' I answer: 'I am a worker like any other, like a
carpenter or an electrician. Only my instruments are
very subtle: only 26 letters.'

"'And what do you try to do with so many letters?'
I respond: 'I just try to think, in tune, with the greatest
concerns of human beings in the light of God; to arouse
in them a confidence in the hidden potentialities within
themselves to find solutions; to try to reach the hearts
of people so that they have compassion for the unjust
suffering of the world and of nature, so that they never
desist from always improving reality, and so beginning
to improve themselves. That way, regardless of their
moral condition, they may always feel themselves in
the hand of God-Father-and-Mother of infinite kindness and mercy.'

"'Was it worth so many sacrifices to write?' I respond
with the poet Fernando Pessoa: 'Everything is worth it if
the soul is not small.' I have tried not to be small. I leave
the last word to God. Now in the evening of life, I review
the past days and my mind is turned toward eternity."

# 10.

# The Different Phases
# in the Emergence
# of the Universe

Scientists today widely agree that everything began with a powerful explosion, the so-called Big Bang. It happened noiselessly, for there existed neither time nor space in which the reverberations could echo. From this singular event emerged the universe. In order to arrive at its current form, the universe had to undergo different stages, which I will here briefly sketch as moments in the history of the planet.

The modern sciences portray the universe, the earth, and life as constantly developing and expanding, as a world becoming more and more complex and self-creating. This account leads us to intriguing questions: How can the Sacred permeate this reality? And, further,

how can or might God become discernible in this immeasurable, incomplete process?

In order to answer these questions, let us gather the
agreed-upon, scientific facts, as they will provide the
foundation for our reflections.

### The Cosmic Moment

At the outset a tiny, unimaginably hot point, full of
energy and possibilities, arose and finally exploded
into an initial chaos of enormous instability and disorder. However, this chaos was not chaotic in the sense
we understand chaos today. It was rather a generative
chaos, because from it all ordered things emerged. It
contained within itself all energies and possibilities
for future creation. After the Big Bang the expansion
commenced and the primal disorder ordered itself into
increasingly more complex forms. This is the cosmic
moment in the unfolding of our universe.

### The Chemical Moment

The chemical moment followed when the primal gases
condensed and brought about great, red stars. Over
millions of years all of the physical-chemical elements precipitated within these red stars and formed
the matter for all of the bodies in the universe, even
for our human bodies. These elements are essential
for life. Without carbon, hydrogen, oxygen, nitrogen,

iron, phosphorous, sulfur, and all of the other elements in the periodic table, there is no life. Many of these fundamental elements still move in interstellar space.

During this period there evolved a delicate equilibrium among the four fundamental forces: gravitational, electromagnetic, and strong and weak nuclear interactions. Without this fragile balance of forces, the universe as we know it today would never have come into existence. In *A Brief History of Time*, Stephen Hawking—the renowned mathematician and astrophysicist—writes that "if the electrical charge of the electron had been only slightly different, stars either would have been unable to burn hydrogen and helium, or else they would not have exploded. . . . It would be very difficult to explain why the universe should have begun in just this way, except as the act of a God who intended to create beings like us."[1] Similarly, Francis Collins, who led the Human Genome Project (1993–2008), confirms: "The Big Bang cries out for a divine explanation. It forces the conclusion that nature had a defined beginning."[2] This is the chemical moment in the emergence of the universe.

---

[1] Stephen W. Hawking, *A Brief History of Time: From the Big Bang to Black Holes* (Toronto: Bantam Books, 1988), 125, 127.

[2] Francis S. Collins, *The Language of God: A Scientist Presents Evidence of Belief* (New York: Free Press, 2006), 67. Dr. Collins was appointed the director of the National Institutes of Health in 2009.

*The Biological Moment*

Much later in this process of evolution came the biological moment. From the explosion of the enormous red stars, which hurtled their elements in all directions, emerged the galaxies, the stars, and the other cosmic bodies. Matter and energy fields became more and more complex, and, 3.8 billion years ago life began as a cosmic imperative through the self-organization of matter (which is never inert but always interactive because it consists of highly condensed energy).

*The Anthropological Moment*

In the history of life the anthropological moment emerged as a subchapter: human life as the manifestation of evolution's advanced complexity. This process began seven million years ago with the appearance of the anthropoids, our ancestors. A hundred thousand years ago the predecessors of modern human beings walked onto the stage of world history. Homo sapiens is characterized by a reflective consciousness, a mind, freedom, and self-creation, as well as by the fact of raising the theme of God.

Humans, then, departing from Africa, have taken complexity even further as they spread out all over the earth, occupying all spaces, adapting to the ecosystems and also changing them, building villages and cities, and developing distinct forms of culture. (Human beings have lived for approximately three million years, beginning in Africa; thus, all of us are Africans.)

*The Moment of the Geo-Society*

Today, we are witnessing our planet's moment of the geo-society, the formation of a single, global society that lives in the same common home: Planet Earth. This enormous process is facilitated primarily through a worldwide network of communications. It makes evident that we form a community of destiny: earth and humankind. It is the moment of globalization; we are living no longer in the age of the nations but in the age of the earth.

*The Moment of the Ecozoic Era*

The moment of the ecozoic era began only recently. The term *ecozoid* was coined by the cosmologist Brian Swimme and the anthropologist Thomas Berry (1914–2009), who start from the premise that we have an increasing, collective sense of responsibility for the future of the system of life and the system of the earth.[3] Ecology—that is, the preservation of the physical-chemical and ecological conditions that sustain life

---

[3] See Brian Swimme and Thomas Berry, *The Universe Story: From the Primordial Flaring Forth to the Ecozoid Era—A Celebration of the Unfolding of the Cosmos* (San Francisco: Harper San Francisco, 1992).

and our civilization—is moving more and more to the center. This moment of the Ecozoic Era constitutes the current phase in the history of our planet.

Ultimately, we are becoming aware that we are part of a universal process—universal in the sense that it goes beyond the earth and the solar system but involves the whole universe.

# 11.

# Everything in the Universe Is in Relationship and Interrelated

We are becoming increasingly aware that we are dealing with a dynamic, organic whole that constitutes an open system. Nothing is complete at its creation; everything is still evolving. Therefore, I prefer to speak of cosmogenesis rather than the cosmos and also of anthropogenesis rather than anthropology.

Evolution does not proceed in a linear manner; there are always breaks and jumps into more complex and higher configurations. It is a dynamic whole that nevertheless encompasses an unimaginable diversity in creatures and energies. Creatures, energies, and orderings are interrelated with one another—as Pope Francis has explicitly stressed in his encyclical *Laudato Si': On Care for Our Common Home* (see esp. nos. 87, 137, and 142). Everything has to be seen with everything else, in every respect, under all circumstances, and at all times.

This connectedness reveals the collaboration of everyone with everyone else. It is the most fundamental law in the universe: synergy, solidarity, mutuality, and cooperation. Everybody and everything work together with the aim that each creature and every order continues to exist and co-evolve.

Natural selection by competition and the survival of the fittest (Darwin) must be understood as an integral factor in this universal interaction of everybody with everybody, not as an alternative to it.

This interdependence and interaction lead to a complementary reciprocity. Nothing is superfluous or "left in the cold." Even the wild herbs, says Pope Francis in *Laudato Si'*, praise God in their own manner: "Rather than a problem to be solved, the world is a joyful mystery to be contemplated with gladness and praise" (no. 12).

Everyone contributes to the majesty and beauty of this organic and dynamic whole. Evolution is, therefore, always co-evolution. Never does a creature or a species or an ecosystem develop all alone. Rather, everything evolves together.

The mutual and universal reciprocity ensures the existence of the systems and their representatives. This means that the greater the web of mutual connections, the more secure will be a survival in the present and also in the future.[1]

The equilibrium, which is at the heart of the whole process, is dynamic and always open to new levels of realization. The reason for this openness is the permanently self-creating and self-organizing character of this process, a process that is always subject to the fluctuations of and the deviations from this equilibrium. In turn, it provokes the search for a new equilibrium that again is dynamic and open. This process goes on and on.

According to Ilya Prigogine (1917–2003), who was honored with a Nobel Prize in chemistry in 1977, life originated from a condition of chaos that was far from an equilibrium; the emergence of life generated a new equilibrium. Life creates what Prigogine terms "dissipative structures."[2] These structures dissipate the entropy and use the natural remains as new sources of energy, thereby prolonging their existence. In the same way, biodiversity points to a variety of equilibria, all of which are dynamic and interrelated.

Evolution is never only the adaptation of everyone to everybody within ecosystems but also involves the exchange of information and experience. Matter and all things are the carriers not only of mass and energy but also of data, for they are constantly involved in

---

[1] See Leonardo Boff, *Sustentabilidade* (Petrópolis: Vozes, 2010).

[2] See Ilya Prigogine, *Introduction to Thermodynamics of Irreversible Processes* (Springfield, IL: Charles C. Thomas Publisher, 1955).

processes of exchanging, assimilating, disengaging, constructing, and learning. This continual process puts its mark on each individual. As a result, all creatures become bearers of history and irreversibility as well as bearers of a certain measure of interiority and subjectivity.

However, the universe is not the sum of all creatures; rather, it is the manifestation of all relationships and connections among all beings with one another. The ability to establish relationships and thus to form entities, so-called fields, is what constitutes the spirit of the universe.[3] This spirit is the main support within the entirety of the relationships of everything with everything. This process started at the most primordial moment when the primal particles began to form (for example, into top-quarks, protons, and neutrons). Therefore, the origins of the mind are as old as the universe itself. Since all creatures are continuously interrelated, they carry, in their respective ways, the spirit in themselves. The *principle* of interrelationality is always the same, although its degree varies. In a mountain it occurs in a rather rudimentary form, but in us it takes a very

---

[3] Translators' note: Throughout these chapters the words *spirit* and *mind*—*espíritu* in Portuguese and *Geist* in German—usually function in the sense of "natural spirit" and "natural mind" as distinct from the "Holy Spirit." However, *spirit* and *mind* are sometimes used ambiguously, as though implying God and thereby blurring panentheism and pantheism. That said, Boff explicitly espouses a Christian notion of panentheism, while renouncing pantheism (see below, Chapter 17).

concentrated, cognitive, and conscious form. All of this points to a purpose and a meaning. In order for the universe to reach the point at which we stand today, everything had to have happened exactly as it has, that is, if things had not unfolded in precisely the same way, down to the smallest detail, we could not be here now to discuss all of it.

For this reason the renowned British physicist Freeman Dyson (b. 1923) maintains: "The more I examine the universe and study the details of its architecture, the more evidence I find that the universe in some sense must have known that we were coming."[4] The purpose of the universe is, therefore, not only to perpetuate everything that exists but also to "real-ize" all of its latent potentialities and those in all creatures existing within it. Therefore, the real is a "real-izing," that is, a continual process, something that is never finished.

The explicit order refers to an implicit order, as claimed by the renowned North American physicist David Bohm (1917–92). Bohm lived and taught in Brazil from 1951 to 1955. It postulates a higher, intelligent wholeness. This postulate brings many cosmologists to assume that the universe is self-conscious and carries the spirit in itself.[5] This cosmological view compels us

---

[4] Freeman J. Dyson, *Disturbing the Universe* (New York: Harper and Row, 1979), 250.

[5] See Mark Hathaway and Leonardo Boff, *The Tao of Liberation: Exploring the Ecology of Transformation* (Maryknoll, NY: Orbis Books, 2009), 168–245.

ultimately to perceive reality not as a machine but as a living organism, not as a finite whole but as an open system and a web of relationships.

The tendency of every being to preserve itself is complemented by the inclination to integrate itself into a greater whole. It is, therefore, important to proceed from the individual parts to the whole, from objects to subjects, from structures to processes, from standpoints to relationships. Thus, everything in the universe is co-creating, co-participating, interrelating, and interconnecting with everything and everybody else.

# 12.

# Our Place in Cosmogenesis

First of all, humankind is part and parcel of the universe in evolution and is a link in the chain of life. When human beings appeared in the history of the world, 99.98 percent of the earth was already complete. Therefore, the earth was not dependent on human beings for the development of its bewildering complexity and rich biodiversity. Humankind is the result of this process, not the reason for it. The usual anthropocentrism—which assumes that all things of the earth and the universe only attain meaning when they are ordered toward human beings—is therefore out of place from the start. It ignores that everything possesses relative autonomy and deserves respect; it also disregards that everything is interrelated and ordered to everything else. Hardly anyone has criticized anthropocentrism as sharply as Pope Francis in his encyclical *Laudato Si'*, in which he holds anthropocentrism responsible for today's ecological crisis (nos. 115–36).

Human beings possess a unique quality; that is, they can intentionally intervene in the natural world. On the one hand, they still find themselves to be part of the natural world. Yet, on the other hand, they face the natural world as agents who can intervene in it. They co-pilot, therefore, the process of evolution in which they themselves co-evolve. Hence, they become co-responsible beings and guardians of the sacred inheritance that they have received from the universe or from God. This is their ethical dimension.

The axial principle of this ethic of co-responsibility can be formulated as follows: "Act so that the effects of your actions are compatible with the permanence of genuine human life." Or, it can be put in negative terms: "Act so that the effects of your action are not destructive of the future possibility of such life."[1]

This imperative can also be expressed in terms of caring: "Care for everything that exists and lives so that it may continue to exist and live. If you love, then you care; if you care, you also love. Without caring no form of life can survive."[2] Therefore, human beings can

---

[1] Hans Jonas, *The Imperative of Responsibility: In Search of an Ethics for the Technological Age*, trans. Hans Jonas with David Herr (Chicago: The University of Chicago Press, 1984), 11.

[2] Leonardo Boff, *O cuidado necessário* (Petrópolis: Vozes, 2013); Mark Hathaway and Leonardo Boff, *The Tao of Liberation:*

intervene in nature itself with responsibility and care by releasing the potential of its existing forces. However, they can also slow down, frustrate, and destroy its potentialities. Human beings can be the earth's good angels, guardians, and gardeners, but also its Satan and destroyer.

We should not forget that we ourselves are also earth (cf. Gen 2:7), as Pope Francis has rightly pointed out in his encyclical *Laudato Si'* (nos. 62–88). We are that part of earth that at a certain moment in its evolution began to feel, think, and love as well as to be responsible and caring. At this moment the human being—men and women—appeared. We are, therefore, earth that feels, thinks, loves, cares, and venerates.

The "father" of North American ecology, Thomas Berry (1914–2009), writes:

> The human is less a being on the earth or in the universe than a dimension of the earth and indeed of the universe itself. The shaping of our human mode of being depends on the support and guidance of this comprehensive order of things. We are an immediate concern of every other being in the universe.[3]

---

*Exploring the Ecology of Transformation* (Maryknoll, NY: Orbis Books, 2009), 304–6.

[3] Thomas Berry, *The Dream of the Earth* (San Francisco: Sierra Club Books, 1990), 195.

The crises suffered throughout the entire history of humankind and the earth system have created an awareness of our crucial role not only in the continuation of life but also in the equilibrium of the planet. By tenderly caring for the earth, we also care for ourselves and thus secure the future of life in general and of our own future within our common home.

Before we turn to the question of God and the related spirituality, we must address two indispensable preconditions: what existed before the Big Bang and the liberation of the "sensible reason," the reason of the heart.

# 13.

# The Original Source
# of All Existence

One question unceasingly challenges cosmologists: If everything began with the first singular event, that is, the Big Bang, what was there before this? Who made this minuscule point that exploded and brought forth the universe as we know it? Astrophysicists presume that in the very first moments after the initial explosion matter and anti-matter almost annihilated each other in powerful collisions. At the end, only one-billionth of the mass remained; those particles that formed the entire universe originated.

How far back can we go? There is the famous barrier, postulated by Max Planck (1858–1947), where our investigations find their limit. In this view we cannot get closer to the Big Bang than one-millionth ($10^{-43}$) of a second, which is ridiculously small. Although we are not able to see beyond this limit, there has nevertheless arisen the notion of the "Quantum Vacuum," which is a somewhat inappropriate expression since "quantum" is precisely contrary to what "vacuum" means.

This Quantum Vacuum represents the entirety of all possible energies and information as well as their eventual designations, such as mass, matter, and energy in the existing creation. Therefore, we prefer to speak today of the "Fundamental Energy," the "Pregnant Void," the "Nurturing Abyss of all existence," and also the "Original Source of all existence," which is the expression preferred by the previously cited cosmologist Brian Swimme.[1] Out of this concentration of Supreme Energy emanated the starting point of our universe and possibly more points capable of originating parallel or other universes. Naturally, this Original Source cannot be represented in the categories of space and time since these did not yet exist and only came about with the expansion of the universe.

Astrophysicists envision it as a vast, borderless, unlimited, ineffable, indescribable and mysterious

---

[1] See Brian Swimme and Thomas Berry, *The Universe Story: From the Primordial Flaring Forth to the Ecozoid Era—A Celebration of the Unfolding of the Cosmos* (San Francisco: Harper San Francisco, 1992); Brian Swimme and Mary Evelyn Tucker, *Journey of the Universe* (New Haven, CT: Yale University Press, 2011); Mark Hathaway and Leonardo Boff, *The Tao of Liberation: Exploring the Ecology of Transformation* (Maryknoll, NY: Orbis Books, 2009), 168–94.

ocean, like an infinite uterus that gives shelter to all the information, possibilities, and potentialities of being that will be emerging throughout cosmogenesis, becoming increasingly complex and interiorized as the process advances.[2] This Fundamental Energy is contained in everything. Without it, nothing could survive. As conscious and spiritual creatures, we are a complex, subtle, and extremely interactive manifestation of this energy.

Could this infinite, mysterious, unnameable sea not be the presence of God? Theologically speaking, however, God is always greater, transcending all boundaries and representations. If this sea is therefore not God, then it is one of the most expressive metaphors for God. Most interesting, the tradition of Taoism relates also to this "full emptiness" when it states in the *Tao Te Ching*:

> The Tao is like a well:
> used but never used up.
> It is like the eternal void:
> filled with possibilities.
>
> It is hidden but always present.
> I don't know who gave birth to it.
> It is older than God.[3]

---

[2] See Hathaway and Boff, *The Tao of Liberation*, 195–218.

[3] Lao Tzu, *Tao Te Ching*, #4, trans. Stephen Mitchell (New York: Harper and Row, 1988), 6; see Hathaway and Boff, *The Tao of Liberation*, xxi–xxii, 30, 339, 386.

Human beings possess a unique quality: they can sense within themselves this Energy that fills them and transcends them. They can either open or close themselves to it. However, they cannot render it ineffective. When they invoke it and take it in, they amplify their own energies for enthusiasm, courage, love, power, resistance, and creativity.

# 14.

# How God Surges out of the Interior of the Universe

∽

After looking at the phases of the universe's evolution and the Fundamental Source of all existence, the Pregnant Void, we face this question: How does God burst from the interior of the universe so that we may at least perceive hints of God's presence and action? This question does not leave us indifferent, for it has to do with our existence and the future of all things. Max Planck, who was the first to refer to energy as quants, humbly acknowledged: "Science cannot solve the ultimate mystery of nature. And that is because, in the last analysis, we ourselves are part of nature and therefore part of the mystery that we are trying to solve."[1]

Nevertheless, we should ponder this ultimate Mystery and consider how we became conscious of it. If it emerged in us, it is an indication that it was in the universe beforehand. Otherwise it would not have arisen in our consciousness, for we are the conscious and intelligent part of the universe. Only we as conscious beings can pose such questions. This is one of our unique qualities: to ask about the beginning of all things and the Meaning of meanings.[2] As we know, there are scientists who hold that there is no purpose in the universe. However, this claim contradicts one of humankind's primal fears, one manifest in all cultures. In this regard, Albert Einstein argued as follows:

> What is the meaning of human life? What is the meaning of living beings altogether? To have an answer to this question is to be religious. You ask: does it make sense to pose this question, in the first place? I answer: people who find their own lives and the lives of their fellow humans to be meaningless are not only unhappy but are also hardly capable of living.[3]

[1] Max Planck, *Where Is Science Going?*, trans. James Murphy (New York: W. W. Norton and Company, 1932), 217.

[2] See Hans Küng, *The Beginning of All Things: Science and Religion* (Grand Rapids, MI: Eerdmans, 2007).

[3] Albert Einstein, *Mein Weltbild* [1933], ed. Carl Seelig (Berlin: Ullstein, 1966), 10; idem, *The World As I See It* [1934], trans. Alan Harris (NY: Philosophical Library/Citadel Press, 1949), 1.

The universe is full of purposefulness, which it discloses with every step of its evolution. If we look back, we can see an ascending line: from the Quantum Vacuum we reach the starting point, which then exploded, from the explosion the evolution proceeds to energy, from energy to matter, from matter to complexity, from complexity to ordered configurations, from ordered configurations to consciousness, from consciousness to the discovery of "God" with thousands of names. To become aware of this continual ascent and progressing development is an act of reason. Yet, the question arises: From where came that starting point out of which our entire universe originated? It could not have come out of nothing. For nothing comes from nothing. It must have come from something that precedes it. This is no merely intellectual consideration but is self-implicit, for it involves the very existence of the person asking the question. This inquiry is born in our marveling over the vastness of the universe as it is revealed to us with ever more amazing data: millions of galaxies with many trillion stars and other celestial bodies. In awe, we ask: Who is hidden behind the Milky Way, and who moves all of the stars?

Enclosed in our sterile offices, removed from nature, or immersed in our research laboratories, our minds can go on the most fantastic journeys and can call everything into question. However, we cannot remain indifferent at the awakening of spring and the splendor of nature, its flowers, the beauty of the resplendent quetzals in Central America, or a hummingbird. Whoever does not admire the breaking through of the sun after a terrifying storm is simply jaded. Whoever makes fun of the beauty shining in the love between two people is foolish. And how could someone not be awed at the sight of a newborn baby?

Out of this state of mind arises the question of the Greater Reality. No one has expressed this better than the astronaut Eugene Cernan, who was able to view the earth from outer space:

> When I was the last person to walk on the moon in December 1972, I stood in the blue darkness and looked in awe at the earth from the lunar surface. What I saw was too beautiful to have happened by accident. It doesn't matter how you choose to worship God. . . . He has to exist to have created what I was privileged to see.[4]

Cernan's statement testifies that we have within us something like a sensible reason or an intelligence of the heart that gives rise to the question of God. This sense of awe means that the intelligence of the heart transcends rational intelligence or goes beyond it. It speaks to us out of the depths of our feelings, from the "place" in us where things are more than things, where abide the symbols, values, and reverential awe that stir our hearts. This dimension is very well explained by

---

[4] Frank White, *The Overview Effect: Space Exploration and Human Evolution* (Boston: Houghton Mifflin, 1987), 39.

Anselm Grün when he shows how God and the Mystery are grasped and translated by the great symbols that inhabit our interiority, as understood so well by the mystics.

Based on this experience, which enfolds the whole universe, we come to the clear understanding that there is a loving and good Creator who drew out of the Pregnant Void that minuscule, smaller-than-pinhead point and filled it with immeasurable energy in which all that exists continues to be and to live. There must be Someone with the highest intelligence, Someone beyond our intellectual capacity, Someone at the origin and starting point of our universe, Someone who continually speaks the word *fiat* ("let it be"). Otherwise, everything would collapse to the Pregnant Void or to nothing. In every moment this Someone sustains the universe's evolution and draws it upward and forward in the direction of a goal, unknown to us, which however will surely unify in itself ultimate fulfillment and goodness. Stephen Hawking's little "question of why it is that we and the universe exist" is helpful at this point. He writes: "If we find the answer to that, it would be the ultimate triumph of human reason—for then we would know the mind of God."[5]

It is the task of science, using intellectual reason, to seek an answer to this question. However, it is the perennial testimony of the heart's intelligence to affirm

---

[5] Stephen W. Hawking, *A Brief History of Time: From the Big Bang to Black Holes* (Toronto: Bantam Books, 1988), 174–75.

an answer that communicates the purpose of God's infinite and loving mind.

The previously cited physicist David Bohm, who is open to religious and spiritual questions, has said that "people had an insight in the past about a form of intelligence that had organized the universe, and they personalized it and called it God."[6] In a humbler way the philosopher Jean Guitton (1901–99) concluded, after a conversation with two Russian astrophysicists about God and physics: "I dare not to name it, for every name is unsuitable for characterizing the Creator without equal."[7]

The most reasonable answer describing in the most appropriate way the possible considerations concerning God would be this: God has created the universe because God did not want to remain alone in the trinitarian Community. God wished to have sojourners in love. In an exuberant moment God created all creatures as an expression of divine overabundance. God created us as a shining reflection of God's love, so that we could serve as mirrors in which God can see Godself. Therefore, we are God's "image." God created us so that we

---

[6] David Bohm, "The Implicate Order and the Super-implicate Order," in *Dialogues with Scientists and Sages: The Search for Unity*, comp. Renée Weber, 23–52 (New York: Routledge and Kegan Paul, 1986), 39. See Mark Hathaway and Leonardo Boff, *The Tao of Liberation: Exploring the Ecology of Transformation* (Maryknoll, NY: Orbis Books, 2009), 188, 226, 227.

[7] Jean Guitton et al., *Gott und die Wissenschaft: Auf dem Weg zum Meta-Realismus* (Munich: Deutscher Taschen Verlag, 1998).

can behold the majestic beauty of the galaxies and the stars and be filled with awe and trembling reverence. Through us, the universe sees itself and can become aware of its sublime complexity. When we are enraptured seeing the myriads of stars, it is the stars that see themselves through our eyes. We are constantly forming a community with them, and they are our constant sojourners. Therefore, we do not fear the dark of night, for we love the stars from which we one day came and that shine over us, giving us delight.

# 15.

# A Prerequisite to Experiencing God in the Universe

## *The Liberation of "Sensible Reason"*

It is not sufficient simply to recognize the stages of cosmogenesis. This is a task of intellectual reason. We, however, want to sense God and the Sacred in the universe as it expands itself in us. For this, we must move from the head to the heart. We must complement analytic reason with "sensible reason," that is, with the reason of the heart. Here emerges spirituality. Spirituality is more than thinking about God. It means to feel God in our deepest inner being.

If we limit ourselves to intellectual or analytic reason, we run the danger of becoming unreceptive to some of the messages that come to us from all sides: from the *grandeur* of the universe, from amazement about the plethora of life forms on the earth. Pure reason, which allows for no feelings, makes us deaf to the cries of the oppressed and the groaning of creation, which we have subordinated to our need to accumulate material goods. We stuff our minds and let our hearts wither. In our hearts dwell the deep feelings of love, friendship, and compassion. The impulses of our hearts give us the courage to defy obstacles and have empathy for others.

Intellectual reason, which is indispensable for the rational order of the world, evolved only five to seven million years ago with the formation of the cerebral cortex. By contrast, sensible reason, also known as the heart's reason, evolved almost twelve million years ago as the cosmic-genetic process brought forth mammals. These creatures possess a part in the brain, known as the limbic system, where feelings, sensibility, care, and love are located. When mammals give birth, they care for their young with tender care and affection.

We like to forget that we also belong to this line of origin. First and foremost, we are feeling beings who are affected by and also affect others. We bear in ourselves the *pathos* that is older than the *logos*. It happens that modern scientific research, in the name of objectivity, looks with suspicion on sensible reason, the reason of the heart. A new theory of knowledge has shown us, however, that there is no such objectivity; every act of knowing is influenced by one's interests. Knowing subjects approach the object of research with their own ideas, their particular worldviews, and their own projections; as quantum physics has shown, object and subject are always deeply connected.

Today, the liberation of sensible reason, the reason of the heart, is becoming ever more pressing.[1] Yet, it neither replaces intellectual reason, nor does it restrict it. It competes with it and makes sure that science is guided by conscience, by a sense of life rather than by market forces looking for financial gain. Without sensible reason or the heart's reason, we could hardly sense God as a living, meaningful experience that sees to it that we have empathy for those who suffer, treat life with respect, and strengthen the life capacity of our wounded, crucified Mother Earth. With that love, which grows out of the reason of the heart, we take a stand for our common home, Mother Earth, becoming and remaining inhabitable for all.

---

[1] See Michel Maffesoli, *Éloge de la raison sensible* (Paris: Bernard Grasset, 1996); Leonardo Boff and Bruno Kern, *Os direitos do coração* (São Paulo: Paulus, 2016).

# 16.

# What Names Will We Give to God's Manifestation in the Genesis of the Cosmos?

When the reason of the heart is set free in us and we are open to behold God in the inner realm of all things, we have the need to name this inexpressible Presence. We know well that it is human audacity to give a name to the Without Name. However, an urge within us has us find names and then even more names, which are just expressions of our love and reverence.

The name that initially comes to us is *First Being,* the living and authentic One who exists eternally, the Source who brings forth all beings. Why does this Being exist and not nothingness? There is no answer to this question, a conundrum with which Leibniz

(1646–1716) and Heidegger (1889–1976) as well as many other philosophers have toiled. This question is only possible for us to ask because we in fact realize that we exist, that being surpasses nothingness. If there were nothingness, we would not be here to ask about it.

Another name for God is *Creator Spirit*. *Spirit* is one of the most exalted words in our language; it carries all positive connotations such as creativity, order, understanding, and light. The Spirit has created everything out of nothing and has set everything in motion.

A third name, a cosmological expression, is *Living Relation*. Everything is connected with everything else, for Supreme Reality is, in essence, substantial connectedness, the community of life and love. Living Relation is present in all things, constantly connecting and reconnecting and thereby forming the so-called *Relation Matrix*, outside of which nothing exists.

Other than as the First Being and the Source of All Existence, God also self-discloses as Infinite and eternal Love—which Dante Alighieri (1265–1321) praises in the concluding line of his *Divine Comedy* as "the Love that moves the sun and the other stars" ("L'amor che move il sole e l'altre stelle").[1] I would add that Love also moves our hearts. As the Scholastic scholars said, love by its nature is *diffusum sui* ("love diffuses

---

[1] Dante Alighieri, *The Divine Comedy: The Paradiso*, trans. John Ciardi (New York: New American Library, Penguin Books, 1961), Canto 33, #145.

and flows on its own"). The universe and the meaning of our existence finds its supreme expression and its greatest happiness in living this love. Grün's reflections on love are beautiful and profound, especially with reference to the First Letter of John: "God is love, and those who abide in love abide in God, and God abides in them" (1 Jn 4:16b). This understanding is deepened in the Gospel of John, where Jesus states: "Those who love me will keep my word, and my Father will love them, and we will come to them and make our home with them" (Jn 14:23). God, therefore, dwells in us permanently.

This love dwells also in the universe. Love is the reason for all things and for the stars to gravitate toward each other and for us to feel ourselves drawn toward one another—an effect of gravitation that draws together all creatures in the longing to become unified.

This love expresses itself in the *Originating Energy* that possesses the highest consciousness and highest personality and that is the primordial source of everything.

This love is the *Life-Driving Energy* that invigorates everything, stimulates development, establishes relationships, and transforms destructive chaos into a generative chaos and impels everything forward.

This love is the *Attracting Energy* that causes all energy and cosmic movements to supreme convergence toward the Omega Point, as Pierre Teilhard de Chardin named it.

Ultimately this Reality, since we have no words for it, is *Mystery*, concealed and revealed, known and unknown, always remaining—even with every further revealing and recognition—Mystery.[2] At every instant and eternally, Mystery self-discloses itself in infinite dimensions that are unsuspected revelations even to God. Otherwise, it would be a static, nonliving mystery, open only to a future self-projected by God.

For instance, in the Incarnation of God's Son, this Mystery became something which God had never been before: God became flesh (Jn 1:14). God experienced a becoming. This becoming is God's infinite, eternal movement. In this, God manifests Godself as the Absolute Future that is continually realizing itself and that has to be continually realized, infinitely and eternally. To open ourselves to this Mystery is to discover the mystery of the human essence, which never entirely reveals itself to us, since it is a part of the process of evolution, an unending project of limitless potentialities and possibilities. The mystery of the human being is taken up into the Mystery of God or into the God of Mystery.

---

[2] See Eberhard Jüngel, *God as the Mystery of the World*, trans. Darrell L. Guder (Grand Rapids, MI: Eerdmans, 1983).

# 17.

# Everything in God, and God in Everything

G od emerges from the universe because God is per- manently present as Creator, Sustainer, Connector, and invigorating Drive of the still developing cosmos. God is part of each process and each step. This is the immanence of the Creator in each creature.

At the same time, the converse is also true: each creature is present in the Creator. While the Creator and creatures are clearly distinct from each other, they also permeate each other and are permanently in community. In this regard Christian theology has coined an expres- sion that is difficult to translate: the *perichoresis* of God and the world. The term *perichoresis* conveys that the Creator and creation permeate each other in such a way that the divine transcendence is not only strengthened regarding creation's immanence, but so that each is always present in the other while not being identical with the other. This presence of one in the other brings out the *transparency*, the mediating category between transcendence and immanence. Transparency within immanence means that the Creator and creation are transparent to each other; whoever sees one automatically sees the other.

This is what modern theologians have called *panentheism*. Philologically, this term is composed of the following: *pan* ("everything"); *en* ("in"); *theós* ("God"); and *mos* ("ism"), a noun ending. The term *panentheism* literally means "everything is in God, and God is in everything." There is no outside of God. Instead, there is a mutual permeation of both. Panentheism differs fundamentally from *pantheism,* which does not distinguish between Creator and creation but regards them as identical. For pantheism, everything is God; for example, this table on which I am writing and this device with which I am writing. Pantheism indistinctly equates everything with God. This is, however, a philosophical error, for then there would only be identity without any kind of distinction.

*Panentheism*, which ought not to be confused with pantheism, emphasizes the distinction. One is not identical with the other. Rather, it stresses the close, mutual relationship that allows for the coexistence and living together of different creatures united in love in a relationship without a divide that separates them. This love that unites everything is highlighted by Grün in the beautiful texts from the patristic tradition.

Saint Paul expressed this pointedly when he said that "in [God] we live and move and have our being" (Acts 17:28).[1] The great North American physicist David Bohm (1917–92) became a mystic and thought similarly to Paul. (Persecuted in the United States by Senator McCarthy, Bohm lived in Brazil from 1951 until 1955 and even acquired Brazilian citizenship.) Concerning the presence of God in the universe, Bohm liked to quote the short poem of the English poet and mystic William Blake (1757–1827):

> To see a world in a grain of sand
> And a heaven in a wild flower,
> Hold infinity in the palm of your hand
> And eternity in an hour.[2]

---

[1] Translators' note: According to biblical commentaries, Acts 17:28 may paraphrase a teaching of an earlier Greek philosopher, likely either Epimenides or Posidonius; both drew on the thought of Plato.

[2] William Blake, "Auguries of Innocence," in *Blake: The Complete Poems*, 2nd ed., ed. W. H. Stevenson, 589–92 (London: Longman, 1989), 589.

# 18.

# The God Relationship

## *The Reason for the Universal Connection of Everybody with Everybody in the Universe*

The relational nature of the universe, which consists of the fields of interwoven relations, points us to the Christian way of naming God. Christianity affirms a monotheism, distinct though from Judaism and Islam. It is a post-trinitarian monotheism. The originality of the Christian faith is to proclaim that God is not a solitude of one (pure monotheism) but the infinite community of the divine Three: Father, Son, and Holy Spirit (trinitarian monotheism). The three divine Persons are eternally interrelated in such a radical and profound way that they form primordial Reality: one, single, dynamic, creating out of love, reciprocal, and mutually permeating. Augustine (354–430), who has engaged deeply with this Mystery in his lengthy tract *De Trinitate*, said it very beautifully: "And so each is in each, all are in each, each is in all, all are in all, and all are one."[1] This is not about three "gods" or even three modes of the ultimate Reality; this would be tri-theism or modalism. The Trinity would be a sum—1+1+1=3—but this is not the case. Within the Trinity each person is unique. The Father is unique, as is the Son, as is the Holy Spirit. "Uniqueness-es" cannot be summed up, for they are not numbers that can be added together.

Herein lies the particularity of this understanding: the "uniqueness-es" emerge at the same time, united from all eternity. They emerge always related to one another in their deep essence, intertwined in a bond of immeasurable, limitless love and goodness. It is the one God-Trinity who exists in a constant process of communion, mutual surrender, and coexistence, a communion in which each Person continually moves toward the Others, and each is enwrapped with the Others, generating a single, dialectical movement, indeed, the movement of the God-relation-communion-love. Modern ecology uses here the expression "the basic structure of the

---

[1] Augustine, *The Trinity*, trans. Stephen McKenna, CSSR (Washington, DC: Catholic University of America Press, 1963), Book VI, Chapter 10, #12 (p. 214).

universe." If the triune God, in God's innermost, divine essence, is a substantial relationship, then this essence reflects itself in the entire creation of the cosmos. The universe is constituted by the interplay of relationships, and no one stands outside of this divine dance.[2]

In his encyclical *Laudato Si'* Pope Francis draws the consequences of the trinitarian Essence of the Christian God, stating: "For Christians, believing in one God who is trinitarian communion suggests that the Trinity has left its mark on all creation" (no. 239).

He continues:

> The divine Persons are subsistent relations, and the world, created according to the divine model, is a web of relationships. Creatures tend toward God, and in turn it is proper to every living being to tend toward other things, so that throughout the universe we can find any number of constant and secretly interwoven relationships. . . . Everything is interconnected, and this invites us to develop a spirituality of that global solidarity that flows from the mystery of the Trinity (no. 240).

Because God is relationship, everything in the universe is connected with everything else, at every

---

[2] See Mark Hathaway and Leonardo Boff, *The Tao of Liberation: Exploring the Ecology of Transformation* (Maryknoll, NY: Orbis Books, 2009), 326–27.

point and at every moment. An ecological spirituality provides a lens through which we can perceive in all things, which coexist and relate, a sign of the presence of the Trinity.

# 19.

# Christ Emerges from the Universe's Energies and Matter

Christians profess that God's Son has become a human being and thus fragile and mortal. In a cosmological and anthropogenetic perspective his reality was prepared for in the course of billions of years after the Big Bang. All of the elements that entered into the fabric of our contemporary earthly presence formed in the red stars. In other words, these elements included the iron that flowed through the veins of Jesus, the phosphorous and calcium that strengthened his bones, the sodium and potassium that made possible the transmission of signals between his nerves and the millions of neurons in his brain, the oxygen that comprised

65 percent of his body, and the carbon that constituted another 18 percent. All of these constituted the cosmic reality of Jesus of Nazareth.

It was Saint Paul who speculates the most about the cosmic dimension of the incarnate and risen Son, even to seeing him as the point of encounter of all creatures that "have been created through him" (Col 1:16) and as the head of all things, who encompasses and unites all things (Eph 1:10). Filled with enthusiasm, Paul adds that "Christ is all and in all" (Col 3:11). Saint John agrees when he says: "All things came into being through him, and without him not one thing came into being" (Jn 1:3).

For this reason Pierre Teilhard de Chardin (1881–1955), who united the Christian faith with an evolutionary view of reality, maintains: "By the Universal Christ, I mean Christ the organic center of the entire universe. *Organic center*: that is to say the center on which every even natural development is ultimately physically dependent."[1] The renowned philosopher Gottfried Wilhelm Leibniz (1646–1716) attributed to Christ the role of the "substantial mediator" who permeates, transforms, and unites the entire matter.[2]

---

[1] Pierre Teilhard de Chardin, "Note on the Universal Christ" [Paris, January 1920], in *Science and Christ*, trans. René Hague, 14–20 (New York: Harper and Row, 1965), 14.

[2] See Leonardo Boff, *O evangelho do Cristo cósmico* (Petrópolis: Vozes, 1971, 2008), 113.

Maurice Blondel (1861–1949), another influential French philosopher, was also fascinated by the cosmic dimension of Christ and, by and large, agrees with Leibniz in what he called a *Panchristism*: a Christ who comprises and conceals everything, a Christ who is the *vinculum vinculorum*, the "bond of all bonds," who keeps all together and leads everything to supreme convergence.[3] This cosmic view of Christ, rooted above all in the resurrection, is perhaps nowhere better described than in an early Christian text, which is part of the famous saying #77 of the Coptic Gospel of Thomas. There, Christ says: "It is I who am the light (that presides) over all. It is I who am the entirety: it is from me that the entirety has come, and to me that the entirety goes. Split a piece of wood: I am there. Lift a stone, and you will find me there."[4]

Restated in ordinary terms, we would say that we are continuously in contact with the cosmic Christ, as when we are performing manual work, such as splitting logs and lifting stones, or during a eucharistic celebration. To sense such realities and to recognize them not only cognitively constitutes a spirituality of the cosmic presence of Christ. In this spiritual context we are reminded of Pierre Teilhard de Chardin, who in *The Mass on*

---

[3] Ibid., 113–15.

[4] There are multiple translations of the Gospel of Thomas, many of which are available online. This one is from the earlychristian-writings website.

*the World* (1923) tells the story of how Tobi on Easter Sunday had no possibility of celebrating the mass in the vast Chinese desert. Thus, he prayed:

> Since once again, Lord—though this time not in the forests of the Aisne but in the steppes of Asia—I have neither bread, nor wine, nor altar, I will raise myself beyond these symbols, up to the pure majesty of the real itself; I, your priest, will make the whole earth my altar and on it will offer you all the labors and sufferings of the world. . . . I will place on my paten, O God, the harvest to be won by this renewal of labor. Into my chalice I shall pour all the sap which is to be pressed out this day from the earth's fruits. . . . Over every living thing which is to spring up, to grow, to flower, to ripen, during this day say again the words: This is my Body.[5]

[5] Pierre Teilhard de Chardin, "The Mass on the World," in *The Heart of Matter*, trans. René Hague, 119–34 (New York: Harcourt Brace Jovanovich, 1978), 119, 120, 123. See Leonardo Boff, *Cry of the Earth, Cry of the Poor*, trans. Philip Berryman (Maryknoll, NY: Orbis Books, 1997).

# 20.

# The Spirit Who Renews
# the Universal Energies

It becomes evident from our considerations to this
point that the universe is pervaded by all types of
energy of varying density and complexity. The most
preeminent and most decisive form of energy manifests
itself in the phenomenon of life, especially in human
life. There is not only life *on* earth. Human beings
in the modern era have shown that the earth itself is
living and is bringing forth life. They have named
this life Gaia or—like the indigenous people of Latin
America—Pacha Mama.

Christians have an image that expresses the explosion of life in the universe: the person of the Holy
Spirit. As Spiritus Creator, the Holy Spirit enlivens
everything that pertains to life. As Grün describes it

in more detail, the Spirit appears as well as the magnificent healing power of all that is distorted in us and elevates everything to its better condition. The Spirit arouses the indignation of prophets, the inspiration of poets, the creativity of artists, and the charisma of the leaders who move vast crowds; the Spirit animates the simple faithful to live in love, solidarity, and goodness with one another. Finally, the Holy Spirit fills our hearts with enthusiasm. In his encyclical *Laudato Si'*, Pope Francis emphasizes: "The Spirit of God has filled the universe with possibilities and, therefore, from the very heart of things, something new can always emerge" (no. 80).

In fact, the Holy Spirit was present at the first moment of creation and was part of the new creation that began with Jesus's resurrection. The Spirit brought about the birth of the first communities of Jesus's followers. The Spirit was never absent from the great moments of historical transformations in human society, or from the renewal of churches and spiritual communities. The Holy Spirit empowers men and women to become saints, martyrs, and witnesses to the faith. With testimonies from the exemplary lives of lay people, the Spirit has encouraged the journey of Christians and inspired them to speak words of wisdom.

Just as the Son took root in the cosmic-genetic process and has entered matter through the incarnation, so in an analogous way the Spirit has become fully immersed in the vicissitudes of history. The Spirit chose an ordinary woman from among the people, Mary of Nazareth, and "overshadowed" her, which means "to dwell" permanently in her, raising her up to the height of the Divine (Lk 1:35), forever deifying the feminine.[1]

There exists an ancient tradition that shows the involvement of the Spirit in the different phases of creation: "The Spirit sleeps in the stones, dreams in the flowers, stirs in the animals, and awakes in human beings."[2] Jürgen Moltmann, one of the most widely known theologians who has delved into the relationship of the Spirit and the cosmos, writes:

Through his cosmic Spirit, God the creator of heaven and earth is present *in* each of his creatures and *in* the fellowship of creation which they share. . . . God is not merely the Creator of the world. He is also the Spirit of the universe. Through the powers and potentialities of the Spirit, the Creator indwells the creatures he has made, animates them, holds them in life, and leads them into the future of his kingdom. In this sense the history of creation is the history of the efficacy of the divine Spirit.[3]

[1] See Leonardo Boff, *Come, Holy Spirit: Inner Fire, Giver of Life, and Comforter of the Poor*, trans. Margaret Wilde (Maryknoll, NY: Orbis Books, 2015).

[2] Rudolf Kaiser, *Gott schläft im Stein* (Munich: Kösel, 1993), 86.

[3] Jürgen Moltmann, *God in Creation: A New Theology of Revelation and the Spirit of God*, trans. Margaret Kohl (San Francisco: Harper and Row, 1985), 14.

When the Spirit subjugates all ways hostile to life, then the dream of the prophet Isaiah will become reality:

> . . . and the wilderness becomes a
>     fruitful field,
> and the fruitful field deemed a
>     forest.
> Then justice will dwell in the wilder-
>     ness,
> and the righteous abide in the
>     fruitful field.
> The effect of righteousness will be
>     peace,
> and the result of righteousness,
>     quietness and trust forever. (Isa
>     32:15–17)

Let us—in the gloomy times in which we live—reverberate with the consoling words of the Book of Revelation:

> The Spirit and the bride say, "Come."
> And let everyone who hears say,
>     "Come."
> And let everyone who is thirsty come.
> Let anyone who wishes take the water
>     of life as a gift. (Rev 22:17)

Creator Spirit! Come and save us!

# 21.

# The Encounter with the God without Name

There is always a second side to things, a side invisible to the eye. And also there is, without doubt, an appeal in every human being to unveil what is hidden on that other invisible side. We presume that the invisible is part of the visible, that what's apparent is neither everything nor does it give us the entire reality, which is greater and escapes senses. Behind the search for a greater reality is hidden—it seems to us—the recondite, often-denied God without name.

Atheism has arisen as a historical phenomenon, even being imposed on an entire people, as occurred, for example, under the Soviet regime, which installed a materialistic version of Marxism. Also, today's culture, focusing on materialist things and consumption, often invokes the name of God. However, it is actually turning to fetishism as it worships its own idols: unlimited growth, a high Gross National Product (GNP), a strong currency, and the continuous increase of these. It is unworthy to call this God, for it actually has numerous gods.

The quest for the ultimate Reality—both radically human and also scientific—is not becoming obsolete. It emerges again today in the encounter with the mystery of the world and the universe. Here it is appropriate to recall the uncomplicated testimony of Albert Einstein:

> The most beautiful reality that we can experience is mysterious. This fundamental sense stands at the cradle of true art and science. Whoever does not recognize it, who can no longer wonder, is no longer amazed, that person is dead, in a sense, and has become blind. The experience of the mysterious—also when mixed with fear—has generated religion. . . . In this sense, and only in this sense, I belong among deeply religious people.[1]

At this point I would like to approach this issue from the angle of persons who struggle to believe in God, even would identify themselves as atheists. We must re-

---

[1] Albert Einstein, *Mein Weltbild*, ed. Carl Seelig (Frankfurt: Ullstein, 1966), 9–20; idem, *The World As I See It*, trans. Alan Harris (New York: Philosophical Library/Citadel Press, 1949), 5.

spect their stance. Not seldom atheism is an expression of a person's unanswered, profound questions about the meaning of life, including about human depravity as manifested, for instance, during the Holocaust in the Nazis' concentration camps where millions of Jews were murdered. On May 28, 2006, at the sight of the concentration camp Auschwitz-Birkenau, Pope Benedict XVI posed dark but correct questions: "In a place like this, words fail; in the end, there can only be a dread silence—a silence which is itself a heartfelt cry to God: Why, Lord, did you remain silent? How could you tolerate all this?"[2] This absurdity causes suffering but does not offer a rational answer. We only dare to say that we suffer with God, who suffers with his suffering sons and daughters.

The failure of answers to such questions creates the empirical basis for a potential atheism but also for a faith that is conscious of the limits of reason. God—though being a kind father and a kind mother—may be the One whom we do not understand. At the same time, though, it is important that we not bring God before our tribunal of reason but instead pose the following question: What essentially do those who profess belief in God want to say? It may be that their experience is shared by many who call themselves atheists but adhere to the very same values concealed there in the name

---

[2] Pope Benedict XVI, "Address by the Holy Father: Visit to the Auschwitz-Birkenau Camp" (May 28, 2006).

God as used by believers. In these cases God is hidden, remains unknown, but is not, in fact, absent.[3]

Nevertheless, there is a precondition for an explicit and expressed faith in God; that is, people must be receptive to the signals by which the God without name could come close, for God never seems to self-proclaim Godself as God. Poets and mystics know this. Therefore, let us consider what they have to say.

The first voice is that of an unknown author. The second is the angry yet religious Italian poet David Turoldo. And the third is a short poem that I heard on the occasion of the death of a friend.

[1]

> A man whispered:
> God, speak to me.
> And a meadowlark began to sing.
> > However,
> the man did not hear. Again he asked
> God, speak to me.
> And thunder rumbled through the
> > sky. However,
> the man did not hear. Again he de-
> > manded
> God, reveal yourself!
> And a great moon shone brightly

---

[3] See Leonardo Boff, *Experimentar Deus* (Petrópolis: Vozes, 2002).

in the dark sky. However, the man
    did not
see it. And nervously he began to
    shout:
God, show me a miracle.
And a child was born. However, the
    man did not
bend over the cradle so that he could
    marvel
at the miracle of life. Desperate, he
    cried out again:
Touch me, God, and let me sense that
You exist.
And a butterfly landed softly in his
shadow. However, the man angrily
    brushed it
aside with his hand.
Disappointed and in tears he contin-
    ued on his journey.
Aimlessly he roamed around. With-
    out further
questioning. Alone and filled with
    anxiety.[4]

God's self-disclosures are in the small signs that con-
ceal and reveal the divine mystery. However, no attention is paid to them, no question is asked about what

---

[4]This poem or song appears in many places.

all this could mean. The result is human loneliness and estrangement from Reality.

The second text was written by the Italian poet David Turoldo (1916–92), who had the motto "to be *in* the world without being *of* the world." He engaged in intense conversations with the intellectuals of Milan, among whom were many atheists and agnostics.

[2]

> My atheist brother:
> You, who search with great longing
>     for a God,
> whom I cannot give you,
> let us cross the desert together!
> From desert to desert
> we are leaving behind all the forests
>     of faith,
> free and naked, in the direction of
>     mere existence.
> And there, where the word dies,
> Shall also end our way.[5]

Turoldo's poem is a summons to overcome all dogmas and other Christian trappings and to break out in the direction of a noble stillness. Perhaps a Creative Light can shine forth from there. It is waiting for God

---

[5] David Maria Turoldo, *Canti Ultimi* (Milan: Garzanti, 1993), 205.

and nourishing the longing for the Infinite. It will not be futile.

Lastly, I would like to share the short poem "Emptiness as God's Presence." I heard it on the occasion of the death of a friend who possessed an infinite longing for God, even though he could not believe in God.

[3]

> I feel a vast emptiness in me,
> vast, as vast as God.
> Not even the Amazon, the river of all
>      rivers,
> Can fill it with all of its tributaries.
>
> I am trying, struggling, and trying
>      again,
> To heal this mortal wound.
> Who can; what miracle can
> bind this bleeding artery?
>
> Can the finite contain the Infinite
> Without becoming insane?
> It cannot. Therefore, I cry out.
>
> Against this death without dying.
> The Infinite implodes in the finite!
> The emptiness is God in my being!

These poems are borne out of a deep attentiveness to ordinary events and the cry of experience before a void that demands fulfillment. These words also reveal that this experience—as painful as it may be—may harbor something invaluable: we are never alone, an ineffable Presence is always with us. Nevertheless, this Presence is wholly mysterious and not always perceivable. We are part of a whole that surrounds and surmounts us from all sides. In order to arrive at this experience from which bursts what we dare to call God, we must overcome the *esprit de géometrie*, of which Blaise Pascal (1623–62) has spoken. That is, we must go beyond the spirit that superficially comprehends, measures and manipulates, and finally draws phenomena into the knowledge-game of instrumental, analytic reason as well as into the expedience of human interests. This calculating spirit thinks about God, but it does not sense God.

We need a "sensible reason," the other spirit, the *esprit de finesse*, the spirit of empathy, of the heart, care, enchantment, and awe. This spirit of attentiveness senses God in the depths of the heart. Pascal writes: "It is the heart that perceives God and not the reason."[6]

Nevertheless, there is a place where we surely meet the God without name—there where love is lived, where justice is exercised, where there is compassion with the suffering, and where reconciliation is practiced. How many people deny God and yet live precisely these values? Behind these values there is

[6] Blaise Pascal, *Pensées*, trans. A. J. Krailsheimer (New York: Penguin Books, 1966), #424/#278 (154).

concealed the living and authentic God; there God is becoming present. One of the most famous theologians of the twentieth century, Henri de Lubac (1896–1991), puts it most fittingly:

> If I am lacking in love and wanting in justice, I shall inevitably stray from you, and the worship I offer you will be neither more nor less than idolatry. To believe in you I must believe in Love and in Justice, and it is a thousand times better to believe in them than simply to call upon your name. Apart from them, I can never hope to find you, and those who take them as their guides are on the road that leads to you.[7]

According to these criteria, which present gospel values, we can say that there are many Catholics and Protestants, but few authentic Christians and worshipers of the God of love and justice. Often they have "God" on their lips and attend church, but in truth they are corrupt, embezzle public funds, and oppress the poor. The God of whom they speak is no more than an idol that does not hear prayers and also does not speak to hearts. On the other hand, how many are those who refer to themselves as atheists, but ethical atheists, and who try to live their lives according to these values?

---

[7] Henri de Lubac, *The Discovery of God*, trans. Alexander Dru (New York: P. J. Kenedy, 1960), 106–7.

They anonymously serve God without referring to God, and God dwells secretly in their hearts.

Lastly, we—those who believe and those who do not—nourish a deep sense of belonging with the Whole in which we are immersed. We are never lost. An ineffable, mysterious, and loving Presence is with us and sustains the entire universe and everything in it. Is this not the reason why we did not let go of our question about God throughout the centuries? Is this not the reason why God always burns in our hearts? Is it not God's coming, the coming of the Nameless One, the Naked One, the Mystery that abides within us?

We are sure that it is God when we are no longer afraid but fight courageously for a minimally human world, a just world in which love and life together are possible for all. This is the foundation for the simple happiness given to the sons and daughters of Adam and Eve.

# 22.

# Final Thoughts

## *The God of My Deepest Interior*

The expression *intimior intimo meo* ("deeper than my inmost understanding") is handed down to us from Augustine of Hippo (354–430). Augustine was one of the most audacious and most anxious seekers for an always higher God, *superior sumo meo* ("higher than the topmost height that I could reach").[1]

The reflections in the preceding chapters will lead us into the experience of the inner God. Yet, this

---

[1] Augustine, *Confessions*, trans. R. S. Pine (Baltimore: Penguin Books, 1961), Book III, #6, 62. Augustine's Hippo is located in present-day Algeria.

experience is not about the kind of interiority so characteristic of modernity and of mere subjectivity, disconnected from the world and the surrounding universe.

The view of the new science of ecology does not allow us any longer to think we are "something different," regarding ourselves as superior to everything else and as the "lord and owner" (in Descartes's words) of everything we can get our hands on. For a long time we have viewed everything "from above," as though we were standing next to God, rather than "from below," as living on the earth. It is to the latter perspective that Pope Francis has called us right at the beginning of his encyclical *Laudato Si'*: "We have forgotten that we ourselves are dust of the earth (Gen 2:7); our very bodies are made up of her elements, we breathe her air, and we receive life and refreshment from her waters" (no. 2).

In this era we must switch from a celestial to a cosmic standpoint. We have come from below, so to speak, as the result of a long process of evolution in which all elements contributed to our appearance on the earth when it was already 99.98 percent finished. This view brings, to say it again, wide consequences that will redefine our spirituality.

First of all, it will bring us down from the throne of higher beings who stand above and apart from others. We are a link in the chain of life—a spiritual and ethical link, to be sure—yet just one moment in the web of life.

Consequently, we must once and for all overcome anthropocentrism, according to which we human beings unite all values in ourselves as we determine the value of the rest of creation on the basis of its usefulness to us; this is a great illusion and an injustice. Every creature has its intrinsic value, has its place in the whole, sends its message to everybody, and lives with us in one and the same cosmic and earthly community.

Last but not least, the earth and the universe are our masters and teachers, for they reveal to us the Sacred, through the respect and ardor we sense when we open ourselves and enter into communion with the Whole. The first and always valid book of God's revelation is creation itself. It has always given and still gives us wise lessons. However, because we have lost the "alphabet" that allowed us to read the messages inscribed there, God—in God's goodness—gave us the sacred books, proper to each culture—in ours, the Hebrew-Christian Bible through which we learn once more how to read the "book" of creation.

We rely no longer only on the categories of transcendence and immanence that are typical in the Greek philosophies, but now also on the category of the transparency of all things for the Divine and the Sacred. We all are eco-centric and interconnected. God abides in the interior of our deepest interiority.

Today we are convinced that there is no scientific proof for the existence of God: God does not belong to the order of things that can be proven. And still, the data of the cosmological science indirectly supports the concept of the Pregnant Void proposed by the religions as the mysterious character of the Fundamental

Energy and Primordial Source of all being. It is in this direction that we must think of a personal experience of God.

This primordial experience is a consequence of our own existence. There is no reason whatsoever that we exist and are here. Yet, we are here, for the sake of mere existence. This fact is itself mysterious. Who has brought us here? Even if we are the result of a pains-taking cosmic process, there is Someone who wants us, who loves us, and even prepares a cradle for us with everything that we need for life.

We can use the expression with which Jesus communicated his experience of God when he called God *Abba* ("beloved Papa"). This is a child's name for father or grandfather, a name that witnesses to a deep close-ness to the Creator of existence—a God, a Father and Mother of infinite goodness and tenderness. Indeed, God, the Nameless One, is called by a name that expresses our love. And, day by day we feel ourselves in the palm of God's hand.

We not only exist. We also feel full of energy and power, whereby life becomes blessed and delightful. God is the Giver of Life, who has revealed Godself as the Lover of the Living (Wis 11:26). From God we receive life with its power and with all energies that make it lively.

The anthropologist Thomas Berry, who collaborated for many years with the cosmologist Brian Swimme, writes:

We must feel that we are supported by that same power that brought the Earth into being, that power that spun the galaxies into space, that lit the sun and brought the moon into its orbit. That is the power by which living forms grew up out of the Earth and came to a special mode of reflexive consciousness in the human. . . . By definition we are that reality in whom the entire Earth comes to a special mode of reflexive consciousness. We are ourselves a mystical quality of the Earth, a unifying principle, an integration of the various polarities of the material and the spiritual, the physical and the psychic, the natural and the artistic, the intuitive and the scientific. We are the unity in which all these inhere and achieve a special mode of functioning. . . . We live immersed in a sea of energy beyond all comprehension. But this energy, in an ultimate sense, is ours not by domination but by invocation.[2]

If therefore everything is energy, if it is understandable, we are filled in a special way with vital, spiritual, cosmic energy. It is through us that the earth and the universe itself become self-conscious and also, in their own ways, relate to the sacred Source of all energy. This energy, which makes us alive, is another name for God and all of God's other, similar names.

---

[2] Thomas Berry, *The Great Work: Our Way into the Future* (New York: Bell Tower, 1999), 174–75.

The statement that in essence we consist of energy points us back to a familiar experience arising from the Greek tradition. It is expressed in the word *enthusiasm*. In a philosophical perspective, it is a composed of *en*, *théo*, and *mos*. It means "to have God within oneself," to feel the "inner God." Now, the experience of enthusiasm is one of the most vital to us. Enthusiasm is the reason why we start a family, care for our sons and daughters, choose a job, and take on responsibility. It empowers the poets to give form to their inspirations, and it brings artists to compose their works. It strengthens us so that we face challenges, even risk our lives. It enables laborers to rise early and to work for what they and their families need. This energy, which we do not control but which overtakes us, is the active presence of the inner God. To cultivate enthusiasm and not to allow life's adversities to weaken us is to keep the presence of God alive.

God reveals Godself within us in various ways. Let us take a closer look at one of these experiences. We are beings of *desire*, made of *dreams* and inhabited by *utopias*. We are creatures of hope, turned toward a future that has yet to be built.

The Marxist-influenced philosopher Ernst Bloch (1885–1977) has clearly recognized that hope is more than a virtue. It is a principle, a permanent source that is always bringing forth new acts and attitudes. It is an inner energy that has us pursue life with new projects, and it impels us to begin anew after failures.

The *principle of hope* is the source of lofty visions, utopias. These are not hollow. They belong to the potential, virtual side of reality. They give life meaning and enable us to walk toward an always broadening horizon. Without a utopian vision, a society sinks into the swamp of corporate and base interests. A utopia always releases powerful energies that support our ideals. It compels us to continue on our way, and it empowers us to accomplish deeds we would otherwise not dare to undertake. The structure of desire always sketches a possible future. Similarly, we understand God to be the Absolute Future, the Great Appeal, the Omega Point to which we inevitably journey. When we give ourselves to this hope and consistently live the principle of hope, we sense God's presence in our lives and in every action, no matter how commonplace.

Here let us turn to look at another possible experience of the inner God. If everything in the universe is relationship, and if the Christian God discloses Godself as a relational essence of three Persons—Father, Son, and Holy Spirit—it is only natural that the human being, the "image and likeness of God," appears as a relational being.

In 1845, Karl Marx (1818–83) wrote his famous eleven theses about Feuerbach. These were first published in 1888 by Friedrich Engels. In the sixth thesis Marx posits a true, albeit reductionist, claim: "The human essence is no abstraction inherent in each single individual. In its reality it is the ensemble of the social relations."[3] Ultimately, human essence is not conceivable without social relationships. Yet it is much more than that because it results from the entirety of the interrelationships of all human beings and develops in all directions.

Without attempting a definition of the human essence, we can say at least this much: The human being, similar to the triune God, seems to be a node of relationships that turns in all directions— downward, upward, inward, and outward. Each is similar to a rhizome, whose bulb sends out roots in all directions. Human beings grow by activating this complex, relational network, not only social relationships but all relationships, especially those headed toward the Infinite. To put it another way, human beings are characterized by the fact that each is an open system, an "un-limited opening": to oneself, to the world, to others, to the universal whole, and to the ultimate Reality.

Human beings sense within themselves an Infinite Heartbeat, even though they encounter only finite things. Because of this experience they also feel their permanent fragmentation and dissatisfaction. These are not psychological problems specialists could treat. They are not defects but distinct, ontological human elements. Human beings emerge as uncompleted projects, projects made of relationships, and, as such, they resemble the relational nature of the universe and the

---

[3] Karl Marx, "Theses on Feuerbach," in Karl Marx and Friedrich Engels, *Basic Writings on Politics and Philosophy*, ed. Lewis S. Feuer, trans. Austin Lewis, 243–45 (Garden City, NY: Anchor Books, 1959), 244.

Trinity. To experience oneself as a relational being who desires to nurture relationships as much as possible is to move toward the ultimate relational matrix that we name God and the Trinity. As social beings, involved in relationships of all dimensions, we have the opportunity to sense the ineffable presence of the playful God of relationships of love and communion.

This chapter could not end without a special consideration of the patron saint of ecology, Francis of Assisi (1182–1226), and his unique experience of God amid creatures and in harmony with the whole universe. Francis spoke, for example, of "Brother Sun, Sister Moon," and so on. In his encyclical on integral ecology, *Laudato Si'*, Pope Francis writes that Saint Francis is

> the example of care for the vulnerable and of an integral ecology lived out joyfully and authentically. . . . He was particularly concerned for God's creation and for the poor and outcast. He loved, and was deeply loved, for his joy, his generous self-giving, his openheartedness. (no. 10)

The biographies of Francis of Assisi by his contemporaries Saint Bonaventure and Thomas of Celano, as well as the *Legend of Perugia*, recount that Francis "would call creatures, no matter how small, by the name of 'brother' and 'sister.'"[4]

---

[4] Bonaventure, *Legenda Maior*, VIII, 6, quoted in Pope Francis, *Laudato Si'*, no. 11.

In his famous "Canticle of the Sun" Francis of Assisi praises all creatures—especially the lord and brother sun and also the sister and mother earth—and unites into a synthesis the external ecology and the inner ecology. He establishes an alliance between the deepest roots of the earth and the farthest stars that become testimonies to the beauty and humility of God, who in turn has become Godself in a crib and also in consecrated bread and consecrated wine. Francis has left to us a legacy that—as Pope Francis emphasizes—is of great relevance in our time. In *Laudato Si'* the pope writes that

> in our relationship with the world . . . if we feel intimately united with all that exists, then sobriety and care will well up spontaneously. The poverty and austerity of Saint Francis were no mere veneer of asceticism but something more radical: they were a refusal to turn reality into an object simply to be used and controlled. (no. 11)

Francis of Assisi lived in a universal solidarity with all things.

Let us conclude with the wise words of the famous English historian Arnold Toynbee (1889–1975), taken from his last interview before his death:

> In order to keep the biosphere inhabitable for the next two million years, we must begin to follow the example of Saint Francis, among the best of

all human beings who have lived in the West. Given the example that Saint Francis has left us, we must follow with our hearts, for thus we can rescue the earth.[5]

In fact, Saint Francis has shown us that we must not be the "Satan" of the earth but the "Good Angel" who protects all creatures, seeing them as brothers and sisters in the Great Home of the Father and Mother of Goodness. It is this tender and familial attitude that indeed can rescue us today.

---

[5] Arnold Toynbee, Interview, *Jornal ABC* (Madrid, December 19, 1972), 11.

Made in the USA
Middletown, DE
06 September 2021

47532930R00096